RIDE

from the

HEART

RIDE

from the

HEART

*The Art of Communication
Between Horse and Rider*

Jenny Rolfe

J. A. Allen

I dedicate this book to Barrie, with my love; to Delfin, my most perceptive, exuberant, fun-loving teacher and friend; and to Maestu, the most kind and reliable horse and friend, who always gives of his best.

Author's Note

The exercises shown in the diagrams throughout the book depict only the part of the school relating to the individual exercise and do not show the whole school.

Disclaimer

Some of the photographs throughout the book show riders who are not wearing riding hats. Neither the author nor the publisher take responsibility for anyone making the decision to ride without a riding hat.

© *Jenny Rolfe* 2007
First Published in Great Britain 2007
Reprinted 2009

ISBN 978 0 85131 916 2

J. A. Allen
Clerkenwell House
Clerkenwell Green
London EC1R 0HT

J. A. Allen is an imprint of Robert Hale Ltd

The right of Jenny Rolfe to be identified as author of this work has been asserted by her in accordance with the Copyright, Designs and Patents Act 1988

British Library Cataloguing in Publication Data
A catalogue record for this book is available from the British Library

Illustrated by Maggie Raynor
Edited by Jane Lake
Printed by New Era Printing Co. Limited, China

Contents

Acknowledgements

I would never have completed this book without the devotion, encouragement, organization and stamina of my loving husband, Barrie. Whenever I ground to a halt, he quietly helped to keep me focused and on track. He understood my vision and always believed in me.

I owe my father so much; no one else in my family had a passion for horses, but he helped me to realize my dreams and always supported me in keeping my ponies. He never complained and was often in at the deep end with no previous equine experience. Dad took me to many superb stud farms where I began to develop an eye for a really good horse. Thanks Dad, I couldn't have asked for more; I wish I could have put this book in your hands.

My thanks, too, to my mother who allowed me to have my first pony instead of buying a much needed refrigerator. Mum, I will always be grateful for your help in troubled times when you were there to ensure I kept my horses – and my health. Thank you for all the childhood holidays in the New Forest, which enabled me to continue riding; my love always to you and Dad.

I have wholly appreciated all the love, support and enthusiasm from both Simon and Lisa; I am so very proud of you both. Your love and care mean everything to me and I love you both to bits!

My love to all of our family, with particular thanks to Sarah and Mike for your love and support and for two wonderful grandchildren, Daniel and Charlotte, both of whom enjoy the horses; particularly watching our Spanish video.

I also wish to send my love to my dear friend Sheila Reed who has always believed in me; Sheila, you have shown me the value of a true, lifelong friendship. My love also to Thelma Terry who was, for a while, a guardian angel; thank you Thelma, for your friendship and commitment, particularly through difficult times.

I also wish to express my sincere gratitude to the following wonderful people who have assisted in the preparation of this book.

Rosalie (Ross) Harper-Lewis has been a source of incredible strength whilst I have been compiling this book. Ross began to read my chapters and then offered to read the whole of the book. Ross, your friendship, generosity, wealth of experience, together with humour, stamina and inspiration have been my constant companion. There were times I felt very lonely in my quest and you would come through with an encouraging phone call or e-mail to keep me focused and on track. Thank you so much Ross and Tony; your friendship will always be truly valued.

Antonio Borba Monteiro was a real inspiration and guide on my quest for the path of true horsemanship. It was a privilege to ride his stallion Falcoa who was an equine professor.

Luis Valenca is a true equestrian artist. I observed and learnt from his calmness and also his authority with a horse. Thank you Luis for the time you spent teaching me a system of training and for showing me the importance of artistry within horsemanship.

Rafael Lemos has taken several of the inspirational photographs featured within this book. I am so grateful to you and your family, Rafael, 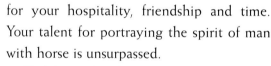 for your hospitality, friendship and time. Your talent for portraying the spirit of man with horse is unsurpassed.

To Miriam Frenk, I extend my thanks for her time and organizational skills which enabled us to meet Rafael Lemos and also to spend an unforgettable day at the Royal School in Jerez. Miriam has an impressive international reputation for sourcing high quality Pura Raza Español horses. Miriam's web site is www.miriamfrenk.net

The Royal School in Jerez has kindly granted permission for photographs to be re-produced within this book. I am most grateful to the School for its generous hospitality.

I would sincerely recommend that you

Rafael Lemos

take some time to visit both the Royal School in Jerez and the Portuguese School of Equestrian Art.

Annie Whitley is an artist with an incredible talent; her works have been awarded several major prizes by the Society of Equestrian Artists at their annual exhibition in London. Annie's work captures both a spiritual quality and vibrant colour. She has drawn the beautiful sketches seen at the start of the chapters. I also wish to thank Annie for the portrait of Delfin, which is truly outstanding. Annie can be contacted regarding commissions through our web site: www.spanishdressagehorses.com

Celia Cohen is a great friend and a talented chartered human and veterinarian physiotherapist. Thank you Celia so much for your input to my chapter: Breathe Life Into Training. Your professional skills will help readers understand more fully why these techniques can prove helpful. Thanks also for allowing us to use photographs of your lovely horse, Tinks. My immense gratitude to Celia and Wilf for assistance with taking the photographs and the loan of a magical camera to help us produce a superb selection of pictures; you are both multi-talented. Celia may be contacted on her web site www.celiacohenphysiotherapy.com

Dawn Williams has used her artistic flair to help me formulate ideas for the cover of the book and also for our web site. Dawn now specializes in developing young Thoroughbred, Arabian and Exmoor ponies using positive 'trust-based' methods of horsemanship. Dawn has her own web site, dedicated to promoting good horsemanship, which is also affiliated to the British Horse Society: www.equinetourism.co.uk

Thanks to both Christine Harrison and her daughter Zoe who kindly introduced me to Antonio Borba Monteiro. Zoe, I hope you enjoy a truly successful and enjoyable career in Portugal both as a dressage trainer and competitive rider. I really enjoyed our time together in Portugal.

Heather Moffat, thank you so much for introducing me to Luis Valenca and I also wish to say how much I have valued our friendship of many years.

My thanks to Alvaro Muguruza of the Yeguada Senorio de Bariain stud for breeding wonderful horses, including our own Maestu, and for providing some superb photographs. Thanks also to Mo Mo, a really excellent horseman.

Thank you to Thomas Osborne for the use of the facilities at his beautiful stud farm, and for his kind permission to ride the stallions and also use the resulting photographs within this book.

Pedro de Cardenas Osuna bred my unique and wonderful stallion Delfin. Thank you Pedro for breeding the horse that so changed my life.

Lucy Nicholayson has kindly allowed me to use the photographs of her riding her Spanish stallion, the lovely Floyd. We really enjoyed the time you both spent with us.

Rachael Forster is our veterinary surgeon with a skilled, holistic approach. Rachael has shown much interest in my teaching and this book; thank you Rachael for allowing me to use your beautiful poem and painting.

Tessa and Hilde Roos contributed so much time and effort, posing for the photographs demonstrating the exercises in the chapter Master the Balance. Tessa is a biologist and centred-riding instructor from Oudesluis, The Netherlands. Hilde is a physiotherapist and sports massage therapist from Heerhugowaard. We enjoyed your company and thank you so much.

Lauren Williams, a national prize-winning dancer, has kindly allowed me to use the photograph of 'dance'.

I also wish to voice my appreciation of Caroline Burt and Cassandra Campbell from J. A. Allen. I have known J. A. Allen as an institution for most of my life and feel very proud to be writing for them. Caroline Burt has now retired but, initially, she helped to put me on the right path; to Caroline, my deepest thanks for your confidence and direction. Cassandra has taken her place and was generous enough to come to our farm to meet us all. Thank you Cass for your patience and friendly advice blended with continued encouragement. At times the task seemed somewhat daunting, but you always managed to smooth troubled waters. My deepest gratitude too to Jane Lake who appears blessed with endless patience and a most wonderful way with words. Thank you for such clarity in your editing which made everything possible. I believe we both share a similar approach which has given your editing further depth of inspiration.

I spent a wonderful week with Henriette and Serge, not forgetting General. Thank you so much to you both for allowing me to use your wonderful photographs. I wish you every success with your stud farm in Spain.

I have come to love the horses of Spain but none more than the horses bred by Silvia Mazzara and her family of the Villa Mazzara stud. Thank you so much Silvia, for breeding such superb horses and your love for them all continues to shine through. Thank you also for the many superb photographs, many of which were, again, taken by Rafael Lemos.

Over many years I have also been influenced and helped by a few excellent trainers in the UK. I would particularly like to convey my deepest thanks to both Paul Fielder and Pammy Hutton. Pammy and all at Talland were so enthusiastic about our Spanish stallions which helped to make our time there very special.

A special thank you to the contributors to the Appendix: Sam Tilley, Bev Clark, Nancy Nash, Gill Kennerley, Lucy Nicholaysen, Celia Cohen, Muriel Chestnut, Silvia Mazzara, Lanys Kane Eddie and Janne Rumbough, all of whom allowed me to use some wonderful photographs.

Thank you to Bob Langrish for the photograph of Indiano XVIII on page 274, to Phelps Photographs for the photograph of Gaucho III on page 245 and to Dennis Bergin for the photos on pages 64, 65, 69 and 84.

This book would not have been written but for our companion, the horse. I would like to express my thanks for their constant friendship and teaching, given to me most generously throughout my life.

If you live in the UK and are interested in more information on the Purebred Spanish Horse please contact the breed society on: www.bapshweb.co.uk

If you wish to contact the author, her web site address is: www.spanishdressagehorses.com

In the archway at the Royal School, Jerez. (Courtesy of the Royal School, Jerez)

Foreword

My introduction to Jenny came from a meeting of two young zoologists in Mongolia where they were studying the re-introduction of Przewalski's Horse to the steppes. One of them had been a student of mine and the other became Jenny's student.

As a result of a phone call, I received a preview of one of the chapters of Jenny's book. I liked what I read and agreed to look through more. As I read, I came to realize that there was much material here with which I could empathize.

Over the years (more than I wish to remember perhaps) I have worked with many horses and riders at varying levels and in several disciplines. My efforts to learn more took several paths finally ending in Portugal where I was privileged to be accepted as a civilian student on the Officer Instructor course of The Portuguese Cavalry School in Mafra and through this experience to meet *Mestre* Nuno Oliveira who invited me to study with him. I studied with *Mestre* Nuno for five years and learned a great deal about finesse and new concepts of collection and lightness. It was here also that I gained a sense of freedom in training; the freedom to observe horses and use appropriate school exercises to overcome difficulties rather than to follow a set pattern of exercises required for the next level of dressage tests, regardless of the horse's needs. Not all horses should be expected to follow the same progression because physique and temperament will vary as should, therefore, our approach. Jenny gives a positive introduction to this concept through her loose-schooling work and with her suggestions on observation and the use of breathing techniques to help re-establish calm and concentration for both horse and rider.

Prior to my time with *Mestre* Nuno, I had been involved in competitive dressage with some success for myself and my students but after this time I realized that what gave me the most satisfaction was working with young horses and rehabilitation work with traumatized horses. There is much joy to be had from feeling the response of understanding from young horses that is only transcended by sensing a return of confidence in a horse which has come to fear human contact. Hence I felt drawn to Jenny's emphasis on discipline with respect born of a passion for the horse. This I believe should be the underlying quality for anyone who wishes to take up a professional activity with horses and their riders at whatever level.

I am frequently shocked, but more saddened, by the amount of gadgetry I see used on horses, generally by inexperienced riders, in a desperate attempt to overcome their inability to control and work their horses correctly. I'm sure that some gadgets can be of use in extreme cases but only when the underlying problem is fully understood and the work supervised by a competent trainer. On the whole I avoid using such things myself and prefer to find a more natural way of approach with students, generally beginning by correcting the rider problems before addressing the horse problems. Here, again, I believe the reader will find much positive guidance throughout *Ride from the Heart*, and so may I invite you to take a deep breath and learn from, and enjoy, this book; your horse will be the one to benefit and you will both get more pleasure from your relationship.

Ross Harper-Lewis
Rierette, France
June 2006

Preface

Noble and proud
Encapsulated elegance.
Hooves beating their rhythm
Rippling muscles exuding energy
Silver mane flying.
Eye and ear focused
Responsive to the subtlest movement
Submissive yet free
Controlled joie-de-vivre.
Man and horse dancing as one
An invisible thread woven between them
A communion of souls.

Rachael Forster

(A poem inspired by Jenny Rolfe and Delfin)

My love of horses was the inspiration for this book, as was my enthusiasm for learning more about the classical teachings, which has involved me in several long journeys. In recent years I have travelled to Lisbon in Portugal, taking with me my Spanish Pure-bred stallions Delfin and Maestu. I found a whole new concept of horsemanship there whilst training with the Chief Instructor of the Portuguese School of Equestrian Art, Antonio Borba Monteiro. I then undertook further training with my stallion Maestu, under the direction of classical *Mestre* (Master), Luis Valenca Rodrigues, near Lisbon.

I can see how the horse becomes our mirror, reflecting our moods, state of calmness, integrity and sensitivity. The nature of the horse will always be to look to his herd leader for security and direction. This is our place in his world and the purpose of this book is to help you to establish and maintain this leadership, by learning to communicate with the horse's mind. We should not seek to humanize the horse, but make it our responsibility to learn more about his ways.

Throughout my book there is a logical progression of teaching for both horse and rider that increases awareness and a deeper concept of breathing techniques in training. The late Alois Podhajsky (former Chief Instructor of the Spanish Riding School in Vienna) knew the importance of friendship between trainer and horse and he also recognized the importance of breathing in relation to the performance of the horse. A short extract from his book, *The Complete Training of Horse and Rider*, on the subject of breathing is included in Chapter 7.

The more we understand about the horse, the less we will resort to bullying and tactless methods in our training. I have learnt that the horse will listen to, and connect with, our breathing. This is a powerful, but much neglected, tool, not only for the mastery of our own balance, poise and focus, but also in communicating with the horse. We use breathing techniques for both training under saddle and at liberty. The rider can learn how to 'breathe within the riding' to help alleviate stress and become 'at one' with the horse. It is the most important tool to help the rider feel both in tune and in balance with the horse. For instance, the term 'half-halt', describes rebalancing and for this the focus is on the deeper inward breath of lateral breathing (see page 151).

Breathing awareness is already understood and practised by professional singers, actors, dancers, athletes and practitioners of martial arts. Many relaxation therapies are founded on an in-depth study of breathing patterns to help control both mind and body, enhancing concentration and calmness. If a rider can learn how to adapt these skills to horsemanship, then not only does he enhance his own performance but he can also become a positive influence on the behaviour of a horse. Breathing awareness is already a recognized factor in gaining personal control and balance but has been rather neglected as a skill to assist the rider and trainer.

My greatest teacher in building awareness of breathing techniques has always been the horse; I am his pupil as well as his trainer.

Over many years I have felt that sometimes too much importance can be given just to riding a movement and technical detail. We love 'to do', whereas the horse will empathize more with 'feel' and 'focus'.

The first two chapters delve into the mind and spirit of the horse and take a realistic look at our human nature. Our horses will always be aware of our moods and body language so within these pages I hope to illustrate the many ways to connect with the horse using mind-to-mind communications. When we are hurting, confused or upset, we may either withdraw and become quiet and sullen or, perhaps, lash out with strong words and temper. The horse feels similar emotions and can respond in a similar way. If we consider his happiness and respect his nature and instincts, he will be more confident and relaxed in his training.

Horses will respect a leader who understands how to make them feel confident, but they will lose confidence in a trainer who instigates permanent fear. The horse is a creature with strong instincts of fear and flight. We want to guide him to a place of calmness and communication as well as positive energy and work. This can be a place of harmony of spirit for man and horse together.

If we seek to gain this depth of knowledge then the ridden work will be a time of trust and mutual learning, and the loose work is a useful exercise to help us to look at the horse moving naturally without force.

Further chapters discuss techniques inspired by my training with the Chief Instructor of the Portuguese School of Equestrian Art.

Throughout the work with the horse, I explain the significance of our breathing and I have dedicated a chapter to techniques to help the reader develop a greater understanding of this.

The journey for me began with a desire to learn and acquire further knowledge about the more advanced movements but then my goals totally changed. I now seek ways of teaching the horse, which ensure that he too can experience joy and satisfaction in his work. The goals are not just to satisfy personal desires but to achieve that deeper sense of understanding.

More understanding will create more empathy and harmony in riding, so that the horse will become your friend and, perhaps, your soul mate.

I have been careful to choose photographs that I trust enhance the feel for art within horsemanship and the spiritual nature of the horse.

I hope you feel this book is like a fresh breeze to blow you gently along the path of horsemanship, that you learn something from it that will help you and your horse to come together both mentally and spiritually, and that, whatever your level of training and field of equine interest, you will find within these pages some wisdom and new challenges. Enjoy the journey.

Riders from the Royal School, Jerez

My Definition of 'Classical'

I feel it is necessary to define my interpretation of the word 'classical' in its relevance to my philosophies and to my book.

I have sought to teach the horse with respect and love and to learn more of the technical teachings of the classical Masters. My journey has taken me to Portugal to observe and learn from such Masters.

We live in an era where everything has a label and 'classical' has become one such label. My own skills are borne of much time observing horses and recognizing their tremendous sensitivity and willingness to please and, for me, therefore, 'classical' encompasses the ideal of working with the horse for the sake of harmony, art, joy and love. Historically, the teachings of the classical Masters give a basic direction and guidance to this journey. My aim has been to learn, understand and teach a logical progression of horsemanship, where the wellbeing of the horse is paramount. These philosophies are equally important for the competitive rider and for those wishing to further their understanding of the horse for their own pleasure and the continuance of the true art of horsemanship.

Soul mates (photo: Rafael Lemos)

Introduction

'There should be no mediocrity in love and without love you cannot create an art'
[my emphasis] Nuno Oliveira

Every relationship is unique whether between man and woman, parent and child or human and horse. There are no fixed rules for success but a mutual trust, respect and love would be high on the list of qualities needed as would genuinely caring for the person or animal and a true concern for their wellbeing.

Throughout the pages of this book my intention is to help you understand more fully the nature of the horse and how we can use our intelligence to connect with him. I want to encourage the reader to rediscover the world of the horse and gain more understanding of his nature, so that riding can be truly from the heart. As our mutual understanding grows, so our riding will become a more fulfilling experience, exploring the boundaries of communication and friendship between man and horse.

This friendship can be one which is illustrated by the Gaelic word *anam chara*, which means 'soul friend'. What is a soul friend? The Druids and monks who formed the origins of the Celtic Church believed that soul friendship was paramount to their tradition and faith. They also displayed a great empathy with nature and animals; beliefs that are still part of the Celtic Church.

The following words and phrases, describe the attributes of a friendship of the soul.

A relationship built on trust and respect. In a world of increasing complexity, in a culture where fear and violence flourish we can build face-to-face communications, from a place of truth, from the heart.

The ability to express leadership and become a mentor.

Displaying the graceful art of listening based on a desire to acquire wisdom.

The friendship demands true humility, yet true honesty.

A friendship where we put down the arms of resentment, greed and anger and find a quiet place of truth about ourselves.

These ingredients for an *anam chara* relationship are also the requirements for the mastery of true horsemanship. This is an art which is in danger of being lost, replaced by artificial goals enhanced by the times in which we live.

I have found my language of breathing and body language to be understood by all horses regardless of age and bloodlines and I wish to help others to learn and use this language to gain a better insight into the world

I.1 Building a bond of trust

of the horse and to build a bond of trust (Figure I.1) It is our responsibility to be aware of the natural instincts and ways of the horse, and developing a system of teaching based on harmony and empathy with the horse that follows true classical principles.

Horses learn by observation and copying movement. Their highly developed instinct of fear and flight causes an immediate transformation from their relaxed behaviour if they sense danger or confrontation and it is so important to realize how stress affects the horse; my understanding of this has helped me to formulate a system of teaching that encourages calm, but responsive, behaviour.

Focus and concentrate — come together

At liberty, the mares in the field will eat and move in unison and will respond immediately to any movement made by another member of the herd. This is their language, which requires much observation for humans to perceive. Humans think, speak and respond with a verbal language. Horses, however, have their own system of communication; they respond to breathing, tension and body language, the significance of which we may not be aware in our world of verbal communication, self-motivation and self-interest.

The Early Days and First Steps to Portugal

Forest paths

As a child I was totally captivated by the native ponies of the New Forest when I watched *The Children of the New Forest* on the television. I pleaded with my parents to take me there. I was only seven years of age.

I spent many solitary hours, sitting quietly, in the glades of the New Forest, observing the herds of wild ponies. I learnt the familiarity of their daily routines, habits and interaction together as a family group. I knew instinctively where they would be grazing at certain times of the day. There was a time for resting, a time for eating and a time for moving on, using the same familiar paths day after day. I saw the interaction of the stallions and the mares and also watched the younger colts assert their dominance, which was often short-lived!

I.2 Jenny – Early years in the New Forest

Those hours spent watching the horse in his natural environment taught me more than I realized at the time because I did not regard these hours as lessons but a time of fascination and absorption (Figure I.2).

During my early years I took part in all aspects of riding including hacking, jumping and falling off. My Dartmoor pony, Monty, knew how to stop in an instant, lower his head and off I came. Then I bought a lovely ex-racehorse: a chestnut mare for whom, in order to ride her, much sensitivity was required, but I succeeded in staying on board, most of the time. Throughout those years I competed in jumping classes and gymkhanas, sometimes hacking for ten miles to take part in a show.

For several years my equestrian pursuits were put on hold while I raised my family and fostered adolescents with particularly difficult behavioural problems. Although this was not connected with horses, the observations I was making while caring for these youngsters were to have a significant impact on how I viewed the relationship between humans and horses. Relationship breakdown often left a trail of deep-rooted anger and despair. I learnt that recovery and healing from a traumatic relationship can only be a slow process requiring much patience and mutual trust.

My deep love of horses began when I was very young and, throughout my life, my experiences have taught me to focus upon each horse as an individual. Training is more than the movement or exercise itself; for both horse and rider it can be an expression of their personality and joy.

When I initially commenced formal dressage training I realized that there was a huge gap between my observations of horses in my youth and the technical approach within dressage. My learning was functional but I felt a lack of depth and understanding; I was not truly riding from the heart. Constantly I tried to be technically correct but my creative, sensitive and artistic nature found this approach rather restrictive. Learning to perform movements to impress a judge did not tally with my feelings; something very fundamental was missing for me. My pleasure came from building relationships with my horses and developing a way of communicating with them.

The Glen Miller band produced superb music but for years Miller insisted that, although the music was good, he was still searching for a unique and more exciting sound. Then, just by accident one day, the band placed more emphasis on the saxophone. The new sound was phenomenal and captured the imagination of everyone of that generation. I experienced a similar feeling. Training horses was my passion but my understanding was too limited; I was not making music.

In the steps of the Masters (*Mestres*)

The Iberian horse was the breed preferred by the classical Masters. For centuries the horses were bred for their specific qualities of lightness, sensitivity, supreme athletic ability and trainability, and an outstanding empathy with man. Today Iberian horses are again being recognized for these qualities.

When I chose to follow the path of classical teaching, the first stage of the long journey led me to take Delfin to the stables of the Dr. Guilherme Borba, nestling as a haven of tranquility amongst the high-rise apartments that straggle the outskirts of northern Lisbon.

> Let riding be art and joy

I enjoyed the warmth of the Portuguese sunshine whilst absorbing the scene created by Dr. Borba with his Lusitano stallion (Figure I.3). Together they danced with one-time tempi-changes and Spanish walk, totally concentrating on, and completely in tune with, each other. Here I discovered the nuances and harmonies I had been seeking. Here was music. This was horsemanship; man and horse together, both filled with an energy and joy that stirred the soul. Riding had become horsemanship and horsemanship became woven into art.

I.3 Dr Guilherme Borba in Lisbon

In the classical tradition

There are only two Classical Schools representing the baroque training techniques, one is the Spanish Riding School in Vienna and the other the Portuguese School of Equestrian Art (Escola Portuguesa D'Arte Equestre) in Lisbon. The riders of the Portuguese School ride the bay Lusitano stallions bred from the stock of the ancient Royal Stud at Alter Real, founded by King Joao V in 1748.

Over the years, Portugal has become known as a centre of excellence for its tradition of classical horsemanship. Many displays of merit and brilliance have been given and at its heart was the greatest classical *Mestre* of the twentieth century, the late Nuno Oliveira. His performances delighted European royalty and the cavalry officers at the Salon du Cheval in Paris and the Cadre Noir in Saumur. The incredible genius of *Mestre* Nuno Oliveira is legendary and today many classical riders and teachers continue to be inspired by his writings and teaching.

Portugal also has a long tradition of mounted bullfighting known as *rejoneo* which involves a telepathic partnership between man and horse. Every movement has to be exquisitely timed to avoid the charging bull and for this a highly skilled horse with tremendous athletic ability and courage is required. An extremely strong relationship is built up between horse and rider. The bond is one of instinct and oneness, combining speed, balance and agility as horse and rider are totally dependent on each other's intuition and immediate responses.

I felt very privileged to be in Lisbon, embraced by the whole Portuguese tradition of classical horsemanship. Historically, Dr. Borba has been extremely dedicated to raising public awareness of the Iberian horse. He has travelled frequently to the Spanish Riding School in Vienna and had been instrumental in the founding of the Portuguese School in Lisbon. In addition, the vision and dedication of both Dr. Borba and Alvaro Domecq created the Royal School in Jerez, which has most recently provided successful international dressage riders at both the World Games and the Olympic Games. The Spanish Pure-bred horse is now represented at the highest competitive level as a result of the Classical foundations of training practised at the Royal School.

Master the balance, master the horse

Dr Borba extended an invitation to Nuno Oliveira to teach the members of his family. This included my trainer, Antonio Borba Monteiro (Dr Borba's nephew and the Chief Instructor at the Portuguese School of Equestrian Art), whose direction instructed, inspired and challenged me for many hours. Day after day I watched him riding his young Lusitano stallions: he would often hum a tune whilst riding, but his concentration was absolute and his empathy with the horse was total. He had no competitive aspirations but he and his stallions radiated joy whilst working with discipline and routine; a living art form.

One of Antonio's most fundamental teachings was 'master the balance and master the horse'. (Figures I.4 and I.5.)

I observed techniques used to commence warming up under saddle which brought about the horse's true submission to the inside seat, leg and hand. Antonio was highly educated as a technical rider but his passion for horses created the art. It was a great privilege to be able to ride, and be taught by, Antonio's high-school Lusitano stallion, Falcao, who had a great love for levade.

Every day the stallions would be worked loose or lunged before being ridden. This seemed to work well and gave the stallions the opportunity

I.4 and I.5 Antonio Borba Monteiro on Delfin and Jenny riding Delfin in Lisbon

to let off steam before the more structured ridden work. This opportunity for the horses to become mentally and physically prepared for their training was so important. The system meant that when riding commenced, the chances of confrontation between horse and rider were limited as the horses had had time to adjust from the inactivity of standing in a stable to focusing on training and discipline.

The stallions all appeared to live in harmony with each other, accepting the close proximity of other stallions when tied up for grooming and always greeting a fellow stallion brought back into the stable after work. Indeed, the only thing to shatter the peace of the stallion brotherhood was the arrival of just one mare on the yard!

I certainly had much to learn as all my previous experience revolved around the potential to ride a dressage test in a technically correct way. This may not be fundamentally wrong as long as education with harmony, for both horse and rider, remains of paramount importance.

During my stay I went to several competitions and noted that the atmosphere in test riding was particularly light-hearted and lacking in stress. I came to the conclusion that the history of Portuguese training for the sake of art and joy has meant that competition became an extension of this, rather than being the ultimate goal in riding.

When the time came for me to leave Dr Borba's yard I felt very emotional as I was leaving behind the most interesting period of learning I had ever experienced. On my return to England, I had much time to think through the training and it was not long before I was organizing a further trip to Lisbon.

Mestre Luis Valenca Rodrigues

I had bought a stunning young dark bay stallion, Maestu, from the prestigious stud of Senorio de Bariain near Santander in northern Spain, and he accompanied me on the next stage of my journey to the stables of classical *Mestre* Luis Valenca Rodrigues near Lisbon, Portugal.

> Be prepared to learn something new every day

Luis has spent a lifetime studying his horses and yet he still says that he learns something new every day. Much of his training has been influenced by the teaching of Nuno Oliveira and Luis has also spent much of his life as part of the Portuguese School in Lisbon. Luis has been recognized by his own country as a classical *Mestre* and you only have to watch him working with his horses to understand his unique skills. (Figure I.6.)

I.6 Luis Valenca Rodrigues with Maestu

I was sitting in Luis's stables and observing several children playing nearby. One pretentious young boy had a girl twirling around on the end of a lunge line. 'Piaffe, passage' commanded the demanding little trainer. He was about eight years of age! The little girl instantly obliged giving very athletic movements, but I did think the boy was a little whip happy! It was interesting that young children at play expected such obedience in their play world of stallions. Then, to my amazement, play became reality as Luis Valenca's four-year-old granddaughter rode past me, mounted on a beautiful palomino stallion. She proceeded to perform passage and Spanish walk as her stunning mount responded eagerly to his little rider.

I found such scenes both profound and inspirational and they taught me more about the nature of stallions, as most of the horses in the stables were kept entire. As with Dr. Borbas' yard, this did not appear to cause any problems because the stallions maintained respect for their trainers who, in turn, showed a deep understanding of the nature of their horses.

In the centre of Luis's yard is the Sultao restaurant wonderfully situated to overlook the horses working in the indoor school. Sultao is the name of Luis's much loved stallion. Apparently, some years ago, this supremely intelligent and emotional horse was giving a display in France with Luis when the death of a great French horse was announced. Luis's wife put on some wonderful music by Vivaldi and Sultao was allowed into the arena totally free, after the display. The emotion from the audience must have had an impact on Sultao who immediately bowed with lowered head under the spotlight, much to the amazement of the crowd. As a result Luis was offered an enormous amount of money for Sultao by a Frenchman who had witnessed the occasion. This was to give much publicity to Luis, his training and the relationship with his stallions which in turn helped to promote his school, the Centro Equestre da Leziria Grande.

Luis has pupils from all over the world and I met clients and trainers from America, Thailand and Europe. One German horseman said to me, 'In Germany, we win the prizes, but', he smiled slowly, 'the training, it is here!'

Once again, I reassessed certain things I had learnt in the past and realized that training is not about performing advanced movements but a fundamental knowledge of true horsemanship. The horse is capable of producing wonderful things if he wishes to work for you. If the time is taken to gain his love and respect with patience then all these gifts will follow.

I spent a lot of time with Luis as he talked through and showed me the logical progression of his training methods. I asked him what meant the most to him, as a trainer. He replied by putting his hand on his chest, 'You ride from 'ere,' he said with his charming Portuguese accent, 'yes, from 'ere, **ride from the heart**'. This inspired me! His approach is the essence of any relationship with the horse. It is a profound love of horses which should be the only reason for us to become involved with their training.

It was the same deep-felt emotion that guided me, as a child, to endlessly watch the herds of ponies in their natural surroundings. Yes, a love of the horse is fundamental to anyone who really has a desire to become a rider and teacher. However, it also became evident that before love comes respect because the horse must learn to trust our judgement as his human herd leader. The relationship can then be built upon this.

Ride from the heart

I also accept that the horse can be our teacher and this book seeks to give more insight into how we can learn from being with horses, both at liberty and under saddle. It is possible to learn so much from our observations of the horse during the loose work, lungeing and work in hand. More knowledge of both the mind and capability of the horse can be gained, which will prove invaluable to his future training.

Most competitive equine sports now take training to the limit. The fact that we are able to achieve these goals with the horse says much about his generosity. We owe it to man's greatest friend to be responsible, kind and patient in attempting to aspire to our ambitions.

My focus on relationships and a greater awareness of our own sense of calmness and leadership should bring enjoyment, fulfilment and harmony, whilst embracing true skills of horsemanship.

Reflections and New Goals

The relationship with a horse begins as you walk into the stable and is developed through grooming, loose work, lungeing, work in hand and then in the ridden work. To complete the picture, the horse should want to recognize our leadership and become sensitive to our direction.

Once this relationship is formed, the horse will become more responsive and tune in to all our movements. This bond of trust and understanding will become our firm base of communication for all further training.

I believe at every level of training the horse can benefit from a system which includes using work from the ground in parallel with the ridden work. As stated, there is much to be gained from observing the horse whilst he is moving at liberty. Lungeing will encourage forward movement and cadence on a circle and the work in hand will help to improve the horse's obedience and suppleness, whilst he learns to engage his hind limbs. These extra dimensions and skills can educate both rider and horse more fully and these valuable tools of training are discussed in this book.

The natural progression helps the reader gain more depth of understanding about the nature of the horse and how he can be encouraged to work with us and for us.

Inspire the horse, become his leader

I.7 Jenny with Maestu – harmony

This book also gives much thought to the power of our breathing, which should not only help the student of classical riding, but also prove very helpful to the competitive rider. Many serious competitors use a variety of techniques to help to deal with stress and a fundamental awareness of breathing will immediately help to reduce levels of tension, whilst also creating a fine-tuning of awareness and focus, for both horse and rider.

More knowledge will create more understanding. Understanding will create a place for rider and horse to be together in harmony (Figure I.7). We must all be prepared to learn something new each day.

The herd takes flight (photo: Rafael Lemos)

Chapter One

The Ways of a Horse

'God has entrusted horses to our care, let us become worthy caretakers.'
Jenny Rolfe

The first step a classical rider should take is to learn to communicate with the mind and nature of a horse. If we are willing to take the time and have the patience to empathize with his nature, the results of our training can become more rewarding and harmonious. Our life-long journey on the classical path will make us not only more aware of our horses, but also more conscious of our own responses and feelings.

Children who grow up around horses learn about the responsibility of caring for an animal; a horse is dependent upon them for his welfare. This education can reveal itself in many other aspects of life because skills developed whilst looking after horses can be used in our everyday situations. (Figure 1.1.) Whilst we learn more

1.1 Sharing timeless moments

about the horse, we will also be learning more about ourselves, which can help us to progress as individuals.

When we observe a horse working with joy and pride we know that he has experienced many hours with a trainer who understands his ways and is consequently achieving harmonious results.

A horse does not understand the words 'I'm sorry'

Can you remember the last time you apologized for a thoughtless word or action? Sadly, we often hurt and offend those around us. If we apologize and say, 'I'm sorry, I really didn't mean to hurt you', we then hope to restore some love and trust to the relationship.

When we train our horses and constantly ask too much of them, we cannot say that we are sorry because the words have no meaning to the horse. It is our responsibility, therefore, to maintain a harmonious relationship in which the horse can feel confident and find us worthy of his trust. The responsibility of leadership is in our hands and this creates an increased self-awareness of our actions and feelings. In our efforts to show leadership, we need to demonstrate self-control in our actions. This will in time engender respect from the horse and he can gain confidence in his own identity. We will be attempting to re-create the situation of the herd, where the horse accepts that we are the more dominant member.

The horse is a group animal and he needs to find his place in the hierarchy of the herd structure. We therefore need to establish herd dominance not by bullying or demonstrating abusive behaviour but through confident and repetitive reinforcement. We will become more confident in our communication with a horse as we gain more knowledge of him and his nature.

Horses are blessed with incredible memories which can make training very easy for us. They will however remember previous experiences, both good and bad, whether from the lessons of yesterday or years ago.

Encourage joy and pride in training

Regretfully, this is also true of the horse who patiently tolerates abuse and misunderstanding; he will never forget being bullied or the person who inflicted this trauma upon him.

We need to look for ways to teach the horse that encourage him to be happy, and express pride, in his work. There is no satisfaction in crushing the spirit of a horse and we must create an environment where the personality of the horse can develop and grow.

The Horse in the Herd

Learning more about the horse in his natural surroundings can help us gain more understanding of his nature and ways.

If you study horses as a group, it will be evident that each member has a position or status within the herd. Some are dominant while others take a less assertive role. At the head of the herd is the strong-willed, experienced, elderly mare, who has a position of authority which she exerts on the other group members; even the herd's stallion has to accept her supremacy. One of his main roles is to alert the herd of potential threat or danger.

From their earliest days, foals form relationships within the group and behaviour patterns begin to evolve. Skills learnt in play become the basis for their responses and interaction as more mature members of the herd. These early days are significant for young horses and, if we are fortunate enough to breed our own horses, the correct handling of the foals will help to form a foundation of trust for the future. As the herd develops, foals grow stronger and begin to exert their skills with other group members (Figure 1.2). I have observed many brood mares who

1.2 Colts at play

will tolerate cheeky behaviour from a foal but if a yearling exerts similar pushy tactics, she will quickly reprimand him. Her ears will flash back and she will adopt a threatening stance; she might even challenge the youngster with bared teeth, perhaps giving a warning nip or bite.

Horses quickly perceive tension, whether from their own species or humans. It only takes one herd member to stand alert, looking at some new object on the horizon, for the whole group to stop grazing and become alert to potential danger. If the herd leader is grazing peacefully and is relaxed, then the other horses will also feel calm and safe. This is something that must be taken into account when training.

The importance of leadership

For us to become the respected herd leader we have to gain trust and take a calm, confident attitude with us to the stables every day.

When I am teaching a horse presenting problems of resistance (e.g. bucking, rearing, backing away from contact, rushing, dominant behaviour when ridden, anxiety, nervousness and laziness) I will spend some time just working from the ground to establish a bond of calm leadership. Once the horse relaxes, he will be increasingly responsive and receptive to more sensitive discipline. A calm mind can accept instruction but an anxious horse may rebel as a result of his fear, and then be accused of showing disruptive behaviour.

It will never be constructive to blame the horse! We have to use our own skills to find solutions to problems within handling or training. Insight and wisdom will give us self-confidence in our ability to make decisions and search for answers. The onus is on us to use our minds to think through the behaviour presented by a horse. We can learn to become 'horse listeners' and 'hear' his thoughts and emotions!

The structure of life within the herd is fundamental to the wellbeing of the horse, and so this can teach us the type of environment in which he may flourish, knowledge that can help us to create comforting and comfortable surroundings more effectively for him in a domesticated situation.

Observations of herd behaviour

I have spent considerable time watching herds of horses and how quickly they respond with speed and sensitivity to noise, movement or body language. In his natural environment a horse would be exposed to predators and, as a prey animal, his fear and flight responses make him look to the herd for his security and to the leader for direction and safety.

Daily, a group will follow a pattern of grazing whether it is free to roam or in smaller paddocks. As a child watching the herds of ponies in the New Forest, I knew that at a set time each day they would be in the same location because their grazing patterns followed a predictable route.

I have noticed a similar pattern with our brood mares; they have a routine of travel around their field during the morning and stop and relax on a high vantage point towards lunch time. The mares then rest whilst the foals play, kicking up their heels and letting off steam. The mares seem totally unperturbed by all this and quietly ignore all the activity. Later in the day the herd saunters down the field towards the shelter where they can expect hay and food towards sunset. Each day the routine is maintained and new members to the herd soon learn to join in with these established behaviour patterns. (Figure 1.3.)

Herd interaction can be observed from the earliest days of a newborn foal. He will introduce himself to other herd members using a lowered stance of his neck and much licking and chewing with his mouth. These are signs of submission and respect given to higher ranking members of his group; a submissive horse will behave in the same way with humans but a

1.3 Mares and foals in the herd

dominant leader of a herd will try to be dominant with humans.

When we teach a young novice horse we are seeking to guide him to relax in his back and stretch forward and down with his neck using a similar lowered neck position and a relaxed mouth and jaw. This goal makes sense as physically it is allowing the horse to stretch the muscles of his back, but also, importantly, it means that the horse accepts his work and has submitted with confidence to our calm leadership.

I have observed in loose work that the relaxed attentive horse lowers his neck and relaxes his frame. If we can achieve this attitude of mind in the ridden horse, he will naturally *feel* submissive. This is where training and understanding the horse go hand in hand. Pulling a horse's head down and the use of gadgets will result in him being forced into what looks to the uneducated eye like a good outline. A tight Grakle noseband, for example, can clamp the horse's jaw closed to give the impression of the 'correct picture' but tightness equals restriction and tension and therefore opposes the true goals of harmony and empathy. If a horse continually opens his mouth, he is telling us that the training is not correct; hence the problem lies with the riding and not with the response of the horse.

Submission comes from the mind

Personal Space and Body Language

It has also been observed that horses have an awareness of distance between them; every herd member has his personal space which other herd members may only enter if permitted. It is important, therefore, that we are aware of our own space when handling horses, the horse must not presume to move into this area unless we invite him. In the herd, if you see a mare pushing a foal around with her nose, she is showing her dominant status. We can relate this behaviour to our handling of the horse. When he is being led, we should never **pull** at his head, to encourage him to move forwards. If you pull at the head of a horse he will mentally say 'no' and there is an immediate conflict. The herd behaviour teaches us to **push** the horse away to assert our dominance. If the horse does not move forward we should encourage him with our voice and, if necessary, reinforce our intentions with a tap of the whip behind the girth area. Horses will **follow** leaders; there is no future in pulling, which creates opposition. We need to activate the hind limbs to move a horse. The movement begins from behind not from the front.

If we allow our horse to move into our space, nuzzle us and push us backwards, he is exerting his dominance and if this behaviour is tolerated it will cause confusion. At all times we need to maintain our superior status whether in the stable, when leading the horse or riding in the school. This does not mean that we use bullying tactics but just that we understand the language of the horse and respect its significance.

Become the herd leader

When we open the door of the stable with the early morning feed, our stallions are expected to walk back to allow us ample space to move into the stable and put the feed bowl in its place. If the horse is allowed to push into our space, we become submissive to him and he will begin to take on the dominant role. Once body language is understood, constant repetition will ensure that only good habits are acquired and mutual respect maintained.

We are constantly giving signals to the horse, of which he is extremely aware, but sometimes we are not! He will observe our every move and respond to what he sees as our mood of the day whether calm or aggressive (Figures 1.4a and b). A horse may nuzzle for titbits, rubbing his head against his handler until he is nearly pushing him over. This is not over-friendly behaviour, this is dominant behaviour. I know several horses who are allowed to walk off before the rider has barely mounted and they are considered to be forward-thinking horses. It is important that the horse learns to stand calmly awaiting further instruction. If you are mounting a horse, he should stand quietly until he receives a further command to walk on. This also applies to any form of handling, the horse should stand still whilst he is being groomed, for example.

I have tried several techniques to help the horse to relax and stand calmly, the most effective of which has been the use of breathing techniques. If the horse appears agitated when he is asked to halt, either under saddle or in hand, just take a deep inward breath. Then slowly exhale with emphasis on a long, deep sigh. Relax your shoulders and release the diaphragm on the outward breath. The horse will respond

1.4a and b Delfin observes Jenny's every movement.

fairly quickly and copy this breathing, which will enable him to release stress and begin to relax. It also means he is listening and is becoming more receptive to further instruction.

A Harmonious Environment, Relationships and Communication

The horse will become more content and relaxed if we can offer him as natural an environment as possible where he can flourish. The following points are observations which may help in achieving these goals.

Leadership
We establish ourselves as the calm herd leader through our daily habits and communication, which means we must be aware of our body language and all the signals we give to the horse. It is difficult to attain leadership until we become 'horse listeners'.

Routine
As the herd structure is based on a regular routine and defined times for rest and play, maintaining this routine in the domestic environment will help the horse to feel relaxed and calm as he will gain security from regular feed times, exercise and the opportunity to graze in the fields. Regular feed times are necessary for mental and physical health and wellbeing.

Social interaction and grooming
Social interaction within the herd is a fundamental part of equine life because horses exist together as a totally interdependent unit. Each horse has its position in the herd and feels secure and content whether he is the least respected member or one of the superior adults of the group. Grooming is part of the herd's social activity which gives mutual satisfaction, relaxation and pleasure.

Acceptance of structure and discipline
Structure and discipline are also important for each horse's security. When

I start to train a new horse, I always begin with loose work from the ground. From this, a relationship can be built where the horse learns to accept my leadership. This work, which is a fundamental part of my training system, is discussed at length in a later chapter. When a horse is loose in the school, it is possible to use body positioning and breathing to control a horse's gait or change his direction. From this we learn a great deal about his responses and nature and can study his movement, which will give us more information and further guidelines for his future training.

Once we appreciate the social needs of the horse we can take a look at his behaviour and understand where things can begin to go wrong. For instance, what we label as vices may be the horse trying to tell us that he is anxious and lacking the leadership which he seeks. It is our responsibility to cultivate a language of trust before any ridden work is commenced. If this relationship is already established, a greater empathy can be developed through training under saddle.

The horse will be content to work if he trusts and respects our leadership and this relationship should be nurtured throughout the many hours spent in his training. As a reward, after a session of riding, I like to dismount, loosen the girth and just allow the horse to stand calmly for a few moments. I then remove the tack and the horse can enjoy a relaxing roll in the sand. In terms of loosening and unwinding, this is a welcome, beneficial reward much appreciated by the horse.

Communication: less is more

It is worth remembering that with all communication less is often more. The light, gentle touch can bring about a significant response when sometimes stronger and more forceful handling can create a battle ground. If when a horse is grazing calmly in a field, his head suddenly comes up and he gallops off, it is most probably a fly that has annoyed or bitten him or possibly a bird darting out of the hedgerow or maybe a leaf blowing across his path. If such insignificant actions can cause such a dramatic response, when we communicate with the horse, less should most definitely be more.

Less can be more

Horses will listen and respond to the finest of aids and we need to learn to listen to our horses and understand what they say and how they interpret our behaviour. My stallions quickly respond to fear and stress and will react immediately. If their herd leader is upset, then they should be also. The trainer must discipline himself to be calm at all times. For me, this has proved to be a steep learning curve as my nature is not particularly laid-back and calm. I find that I need to concentrate my thoughts seriously before I work with the stallions. Many people ride to dispense with the daily cares of life and leave their problems behind for a while. It is, however, more important to become disciplined enough to push the problems into the background *before* working with the horse. It becomes easy to understand why learning the art of classical training is a life-long journey; we can learn much about the nature of the horse along the way but we will also learn a lot about our own personalities, which can at times be quite revealing!

One of our goals is to achieve sensitivity in our communication but when the horse checks us out and shows unacceptable behaviour, we must be prepared to demonstrate our leadership and reprimand him. This is a basic herd response which is understood by the horse. Often a harsh tone of voice accompanied by a more dominant body position will be effective.

Horses respond very quickly to our breathing patterns, a fact which directs us towards the use of breathing techniques in training. We know that the horse depends on his keen senses of hearing and smell for his survival in the wild. Humans tend to put more focus on verbal communications than body language. This is why we depend less on our other sensory skills and more on our highly developed verbal language and, hopefully, listening!

When giving a client a lesson on the lunge, I will encourage them to relax and half close their eyes in order to relax the muscles around the eyes. When the rider is not relying on 'sharp' focus this promotes a change of consciousness and enhances an awareness of body and motion. The power of listening to music, concentration on breathing and half-closed eyes can help to bring about a real empathy between rider and horse. My horses will often pick up the rhythm of guitar music playing in the background when I ride, and they seem to enjoy the classical music we play in the stables all day long. I would add that Maestu, my bay stallion, loves to pick up a rhythm with a powerful beat, which I think stimulates his rather laid-back nature.

Our relationship with a horse does not begin in the saddle but at the stable door

When we take a few steps back from our busy lives, we can recapture these sensory skills and become more aware of our horses and, in turn, become more conscious of the signals that we give, whether by body language, voice or breathing. Our relationship with a horse does not begin in the saddle, but at the stable door (Figure 1.5).

When things go wrong

It is a sad fact of life that very many human and equine partnerships end up with a serious lack of communication which can present all kinds of problems. We are quick to label any disruptive behaviour in the stable as vices and a horse displaying these vices as a weaver, wind-sucker or crib-biter. This is the point where, if we wish to understand the mind of the horse, we need to take a step back and consider why bad habits are forming. When any creature is taken too far away from the way of life that nature intended, it might not be able to adapt.

Western civilization is in danger of putting excess and constant stress on mankind to live in a way that causes physical and mental strain. We are under such pressure to succeed, to standards set by our society, that

1.5 The relationship starts at the stable door

we may be guilty of inflicting similar conditions on our horses.

I have seen very talented horses that make exceptional progress in training, but are then rushed in their work in order to fulfil owners' ambitions as cups begin to adorn the shelves. Slowly, problems begin to arise as the horse shows signs of stress either mentally or physically. The horse cannot say to us in our language, 'Slow down, I need more time. I do not understand why I am in the stable all day and night. I do not understand why I never seem to please you. I do not know why I cannot live with my friends and enjoy the sun on my back in the field.'

We are accountable for signs of anxiety and fatigue in our horses. Horses may cope with stressful situations in a hundred different ways and what we call vices are often simply signs of a horse's fear, insecurity and apprehension. A lack of horsemanship can create a negative environment where the horse may not be relaxed or content within his surroundings.

Many hours standing in a stable is a fate endured by many horses who are too valuable to be allowed the pleasure of living in a more natural way. Only God can make a tree and only God can make a horse. The same God has entrusted horses to our care and in return we have ample reward from their undivided loyalty and unique spiritual nature. To have empathy with a horse is to be rich indeed.

We may observe negative behaviour if a horse is lacking companionship as his instinct is that of the herd, relying on social interaction for his security. A herd animal is not designed for solitary confinement in a stable. Horses have high energy levels when fit and healthy and their frustration with captivity must at times be overwhelming, which might cause them to chew wood, kick, bite or weave. If his handler then shouts at him to stop him misbehaving, this adds to the anxiety and unhappiness.

If a horse is relaxed and happy he will have a good appetite and his ears will twitch backwards and forwards as he shows an interest in what is going on around him. Sometimes his eyes may look a little glazed, his lower lip may droop and he will sleep whilst standing up. The horse will be calm to handle and look forward to being turned out in the field where he may choose to graze or just survey the scene. A person can also feel something soothing and timeless by just watching horses grazing and so we should not deprive a horse of enjoying this peace and tranquility as well.

If the horse is not relaxed and happy with his lifestyle, he may show his displeasure in becoming more difficult to ride. It is too easy to find fault with the horse when, in his anxiety, he may snatch at the bit or become unsteady in his neck and head carriage. This is the time when the unthinking rider puts a stronger bit in his mouth or may resort to using draw reins or other gadgets instead of addressing the cause of the problem. Most horses that are tight-lipped and resistant have a problem, but the problem is more likely to be rooted in their minds than have anything to do with their mouths!

Gadgets don't fix the mind

Draw reins, for example, are gadgets that might fix a horse in a position of submission and make him look physically correct for his level of training but the horse will not be feeling this way. Although some useful muscles may have been built up when the draw reins are removed, it is likely that there may also be some mental resistance of the rider. Experience has taught me that time and patience reap long-term rewards and short-term fixes with gadgets are exactly that!

When serious problems arise in training and the horse continues to show stress and a lack of contentment, we must ensure that he is not suffering any pain or discomfort which might prevent him from enjoying his work.

The horse's fear and flight instinct might surface if problems arise when a horse works sullenly or puts on the brakes and says, 'No, I am not interested in pleasing you'. The rider then needs to go back to the beginning. A horse can become work-shy and sour through a build-up of negative memories often involving either physical or mental pain. Physical pain can be brought about by working for too long when muscles are not ready, or by introducing exercises with which the horse is not physically prepared to cope. A past history of injury and trauma may cause problems of communication and stress can be inflicted when a rider does not listen to the signals the horse is giving. He may be too obsessed by thoughts of ambition and producing results with only his personal achievements in mind. By nature, the horse is active, energetic, responsive and inquisitive and should enjoy the process of his training and relationship with his rider. In my experience, it is difficult to teach a horse anything worthwhile if he is really stressed.

Let us look at another example: a tense horse becomes unsettled and will not consistently take a contact with the bit. I have seen riders forcing a contact on the horse and when he resists this and becomes unsteady and tight in his neck, the rider puts on more pressure with the hands. We **cannot force a submissive response** and the unsteady head and neck can become a habit which is hard to change. Again, the problem lies with a lack of thought and empathy. The problem manifests itself in the horse fighting against the hand but the cause is that the horse is feeling threatened and forced to co-operate, which does not make for harmony.

Several horses have come to me with these problems and, initially, I observe them at liberty in the school, or on the lunge. I will look for signs of tension such as stilted or rushed gaits or an unsteady head and neck carriage. I will try to assess the mood of the horse and determine how well equipped he is mentally and physically for future training. When I listen to the horse and then he begins to listen to me, our first communication bond has been initiated. He will then begin to respect a herd leader and his submission to this authority will follow.

Sometimes a horse will assert a strong personality by testing a rider's skills. If this happens, the rider has to maintain his dominance and assert his own abilities if he is to maintain his position as herd leader. This is why we need a plethora of skills at our disposal. We can only respond to behaviour problems correctly if we understand the reason for them.

Anxious horses respond well to a soothing voice and our voice tone is important when giving commands. We also need structured discipline to help them to feel secure. Much stress can be caused because the horse is sensitive and is trying so hard to please but he is not sure of his boundaries and may be receiving confused messages.

Symptoms of Anxiety in Horses

Characteristics and habits seen in horses suffering from anxiety may be as follows.

In the stable
* Pacing round and round the stable.
* Weaving.
* Crib-biting and/or wind-sucking.
* Lack of appetite.

- Tight lipped with ears back.
- Looking tucked up.

During ridden work

- Lack of acceptance of the bit and contact.
- Inability to stand calmly whilst the rider mounts.
- Tightness in the mouth and jaw with no relaxed, moist 'mouthing', i.e. a gentle chomping of the bit.
- Tightness in the neck. The correct working posture is one of the top line stretching up and out from the withers to a submissive poll and head carriage. The lower neck muscles should be relaxed and loose.
- A back that is 'tight' and tense. Movements are stilted and the gaits are not forward and free.
- A lack of rhythm in the gaits, which is often caused by the horse having an unsettled mind.
- Rearing: this can be the result of harsh hands or aids, the use of gadgets, a lack of communication and asking too much too soon.
- Bucking: this may just be high spirits, but can be caused by a soured mind or physical discomfort and pain.

Our training methods using the work from the ground allow the horse time to be excessively energetic without causing confrontation under saddle (Figure 1.6).

Throughout this book we will continue to look at ways of training to increase harmony, so that our horses will not be working under threat or stress but will allow their joy and pride to become part of the training (Figures 1.7a and b). Technically we will be striving for certain goals but the most fundamental aim will always be to keep the horse enjoying his work with acceptance and trust in our leadership.

Practise 'horse listening'

If we **allow our horses to become our teachers**, then we are on the path to becoming true horsemen.

As equine trainers we undertake a great responsibility but, in doing so, we stand to gain the most precious reward of our horses giving us unstinting loyalty and friendship.

1.6 Delfin demonstrates his joy in a brilliant expressive trot

Repeated actions become habits — habits become second nature — second nature becomes a way of thinking — a way of thinking can become a way of life.

1.7a and b Our stallions express their joy and pride at liberty

The horse is our mirror (photo: Rafael Lemos)

Chapter Two

The Influence of Human Nature

'Horses, a gift from God, will mirror our own personalities
and become our best teachers.'
Jenny Rolfe

Can you remember listening to the initial chords of a piece of music on the radio? How many notes did you hear before you recognized the melody? Was your mind transported from everyday thoughts to a tune that you love, or a moment in time? What were your thoughts before the music began? The sound of music has momentarily changed your way of thinking and stimulated a totally different feeling. This ability to redirect our thoughts and feelings will be invaluable to us when working with our horses.

Western civilization demands a very structured, self-motivated and, at times, technical mind to cope with the changes and pressures of our way of life. People are in danger of losing basic spirituality and feelings, which keep us in tune with our own natural rhythms and individuality. The work place can demand a façade of mechanical smiles and responses which do not genuinely reflect the true feelings of the individual. This all takes us away from our true self and I believe causes many physical and emotional health problems. Time is precious and also time is money, therefore many of us can fall into the trap of never having enough time for our own calmness and contemplation.

I have been reading about the life of the Native Americans and how their land and lifestyle have been eroded leaving them to face many physiological problems. Many could not adapt to our 'civilized' way of life. Like the feral horses with whom they shared their lives, their spiritual nature was nomadic and restless and often they struggled for existence. The horses were not just fed twice a day and ridden for pleasure but were an integral part of the tribe; thus the Native Americans came to understand the nature of the horse because their lives were so mutually dependant and connected. This connection enabled man and horse to be in total harmony with nature. The horse is more than worthy of this special place in the life of mankind, but we may not have the time to understand how much more the horse has to offer.

Nations continue to seek the materialistic wealth of the Western world, but these are not necessarily the ingredients for happiness: we may also desire strength of spirituality, a fundamental belief in God and a love for family and fellowship. Within the poorer nations we can still see the genuine smile that comes from within, not just the mouth. This is the smile which emanates from the eyes. The media would lead us to believe that our happiness must come from owning the latest fashion in clothes, cars or electronics but these goals can be short lived if we cannot feel in tune with our true nature or be involved with loving and caring relationships.

> The horse is looking for a leader and a friend who understands his language

When we introduce horses into our lives, what do we have to offer them? Is it lavish stabling or the latest fashion in rugs and stableware? Is the horse in danger of becoming a fashion statement? We all need to think deeply and honestly about their needs if we truly seek to become good horsemen and women. The horse requires good food, grazing and management but, in essence, he will be seeking to experience our true feelings and an environment in which he may flourish. The horse looks to a leader and friend who understands something of his natural language.

He does not seek to be humanized. A horse comes with his own genetics, thoughts and instincts.

How would we answer the following fundamental questions? 'Why do we want to buy a horse?' 'Why are we interested in training a horse?' 'Why do we seek to fulfil our ambitions with our horses?' The answers should be that we want to care for the horse and develop a firm bond of friendship with him. This may lead us to pursue further goals but not at the expense of our relationship.

I believe that our horses do mirror our personalities, which places the responsibility of training and leadership totally with us (Figure 2.1). It is good to learn how our individual nature may influence the horse but this journey can take a lifetime.

I have spent many hours watching great trainers and riders, as we all do if we aspire to further our learning, but what are their secrets and how can we follow in their footsteps? Most of them have a natural empathy with the horse combined with the skills of communication and an ability to listen. They possess gifts of leadership with tact and discipline combined with kindness and generosity.

Listening to music can change our mood by calming us and, perhaps, by taking our minds to a more spiritual level, so how may we develop the

2.1 Delfin becomes Jenny's mirror

ability to change the level of our minds to help in our communication with a horse? When we fill our thoughts with technical goals alone, the mind is on a level of intense concentration and the spiritual side of our nature is diminished. If we are able to keep in tune with our deeper senses of 'feel' and calmness, it is possible to enter a certain 'place for our mind' when riding. This state, if developed each day, will become a pattern for riding, from which man and horse will benefit. In the last chapter the point was made that regularly practised habits, good or bad, can become, over time, a way of life.

Great horseman all have a passion for their art and horses and are dedicated to the pilgrimage of learning. We will make mistakes in our judgement and training, but if our motives are in the best interest of the horse, then the problems can be overcome.

Many comments have been aired on rider position and training methods but I have come to the conclusion that the greatest and most important gift

Find your inner calm

for the classical rider is a love and passion for the horse. Technical knowledge is extremely important but so is a calm determination together with focus of energy. A sense of feel and purpose may help to create the difference between riding correct movements and the ability to dance with your horse.

When Dr. Guilherme Borba and Luis Valenca Rodrigues work with their stallions they are like artists with their horses. To observe Dr. Borba riding was to experience the same feeling as when looking at a great painting or other work of art. He had complete empathy and appeared to have no problem with total balance and harmony which, for the onlooker, was an amazing spiritual experience. To observe a horse 'dancing' in 'oneness' with the rider evoked, in me, emotion as this was the goal I sought.

Luis Valenca Rodrigues would immediately soothe an anxious horse with his deep, guttural, 'arrrh', followed by a deep sigh. I do not imagine he needed to think about his communication, it simply came naturally for him. He always emphasized that you should never be in a hurry when you are working with the horse as he will sense your tension. We have to seek calmness for ourselves and transmit these feelings to our horses. It is impossible to teach a horse calmness and discipline, with energy, when we are feeling totally overwhelmed by the everyday pressures of life. Our sensitivity will reap a quiet, listening response, but our stress will promote fear and anxiety in the horse.

It must be the greatest test for us all to take a quiet and patient nature to the stables. Our thoughts need to be in a place that allows us to have common ground with the horse.

Imagine the following scene and see how it might transform your feelings. Think of a warm, balmy evening in Portugal, walking along the cliff tops with the sun setting on the horizon. The heat of the day is slowly passing and you can hear the waves gently lapping on the shore. The colours of the sunset fill your mind with tranquility and contentment. Can you imagine this scene and the peace you would be feeling? This calmness is the mood that should be taken to the stable in order to convey friendship and empathy to the horses and is the place from where positive energy can be produced to direct the horse in a kind, encouraging and meaningful way.

The process of learning for the human requires a calm, yet focused mind and the same is true for the horse because if his natural fear and flight instinct are provoked, his mind and body will become tense. His immediate response will be to try to escape from his situation. We will not be transmitting the signals to generate the harmony that we are seeking.

Horses may be used, at times, to show off the skill of the rider. The result can sometimes display an arrogance which is fuelled by open-mouthed spectators absorbing spectacular movements. The relationship with the horse is not paramount. This is akin to showing off your skills at the expense of a friend or partner, who feels patronized and is made to feel or look inadequate. There can never be a great rider without a great horse. A great horse will look athletic and noble and perform with true joy and pride. These are the gifts that the horse offers and they are so much more important than just tricks and movements.

When I look at footage or photographs of the great Nuno Oliveira, I see calmness, energy with empathy and a totally focused connection with his horse (Figure 2.2).

The legendary Reiner Klimke always appeared to truly understand the mind of the horse and be full of love and admiration for his horses. His amazing competitive record of winnings, most certainly did nothing

2.2 Classical *Mestre* Nuno Oliveira

to diminish these philosophies. I believe he was firstly a true horseman and secondly a highly successful competitor.

Thoughts on the Ability to 'Feel'

It is a human trait to be in control of each aspect of our lives and the concept of 'letting go' or 'time for stillness of the mind' has been overtaken by today's demanding lifestyle. We all attempt to mould our personality into the way of life which has become the norm and yet I feel that many of us would be more comfortable with a lifestyle where less is more.

If you watch a pianist's fingers flowing over the keyboard, the music sometimes requires a stronger 'touch' but not heavy hands. Frequently, when you are doing something like driving a car, you can become aware that you are not holding the wheel in a light manner but clutching it with totally rigid hands as if suspended from a cliff edge. Our stressful lives often mean that we spend more time 'doing' than 'feeling'.

If you tune a guitar, for example, there is such a minute difference in the tension of the string between a note sounding flat and out of tune and the note totally in tune, which defines the subtlety of true beauty and music. It is the same with horses; sometimes we only need to make small changes to make the difference. If we lose our patience and become too strong in our communications, it will have a negative effect.

During a clinic, I was trying to describe to a Dutch client the feeling between the rider's hands and the horse's mouth. I used the word 'vibration' to describe the communication. Her interpretation of this statement was to direct her thoughts to a large machine repairing the road! I took a deep breath and had to rethink how to get my idea across.

Later I asked her to watch the strings when I played my guitar. When the strings were still, there was no music but a light caress of the fingers created a resonance through the strings and music began to flow; this was the gentle feel I had meant by 'vibration'. We both smiled and acknowledged how easy it can be to misinterpret a message.

It is a similar thing to the difference between learning to drive and being an accomplished driver. When learning, your hand fumbles for the hand brake and your foot attempts to land on the accelerator and finds the brake pedal instead. Nothing about driving appears to be easy; every action from steering to looking in the mirror has to be thought through with accuracy and speed. Slowly, through experience and practice, the foot automatically pushes down on the correct pedal and the steering becomes second nature. Very soon you can drive the car almost without thinking as your mind has processed the activity and you respond automatically.

Mistakes are a part of learning

This is how we teach ourselves and our horses, initially we may be a little strong and clumsy, without balance and freedom of motion but, slowly the process becomes second nature and we begin to ride in balance, more aware of our breathing and posture. Each transition will become a pleasure for him when he learns to respond to the lightest of aids, even a breath. Strong, unyielding instructions will cause stress and the horse will lose his freedom in mind and spirit, the retention of which is the true art of training. If the rider's mind is full of too many technical details, the flow of energy needed to create movement will be lost.

If dancers are studied as they move around the floor, it will become obvious which couples show empathy and move as one and those that may be technically correct but lack the smooth flow of artistry (Figure 2.3).

What are your Motives?

It is interesting to look at human nature and our motives for working with horses. Some people just have a passion for horses and others strive for competitive goals. The desire to please judges and gain awards should certainly not create problems in training providing the

2.3 Artistry in dance

fundamental aims are the love and respect for the horse. Complications arise when riders have to make difficult choices and practise dressage test movements in a sequence that may not be particularly beneficial to the long-term training objectives. The stress caused by competition can detract from the calm relationship and the horse may have difficulty in understanding the reasons why. It can be all too easy to ask for that little bit extra from a horse showing talent, whether in dressage, jumping or eventing. The horse may initially feel confident in his work and demonstrate ability but the competition world can be demanding and may not suit the nature of some horses.

There are horses, however, who thrive on the opportunity to demonstrate showmanship and adapt well to more pressure. It is, therefore, of fundamental importance that we observe the horse for signs of stress and try to understand his responses and behaviour.

From an early age we are encouraged to become competitive and are praised for our achievements but can be scorned for our mistakes. In reality, however, learning will lead us through mistake after mistake in our quest for success. Maybe we should all adopt a more positive and encouraging attitude; all too often we find that there can be a self-righteous, critical response. It is but human nature to, at times, seek to gain confidence through the failure of others. We all have to aspire to our own destiny, which does not necessarily include the approval of others. If we are true to our inner self and convictions, we will include love and patience in our quest and then our destiny through life will be fulfilled. Each of us has much to learn and something to give, we owe it to ourselves to use the gifts that we have been given. These can be used just for personal progress or may be shared to encourage others in their quest for understanding.

Progressing our Techniques

If we seek to become teachers and riders of classical equitation, we need to form an understanding of human nature and how we can relate to our horses. It is all too easy to be totally unaware of our influence on horses' minds. They observe everything including our mood, body language and tone of voice and all these impart different messages to our horses.

By understanding the effect of tension on horses, the aspiring rider can learn much which is helpful in the more stressed, competitive environment. It can be extremely difficult to control nerves and also have the responsibility of relaxing the horse in such a situation. This can be improved as horse and rider gain more experience at 'training' under the public eye and breathing techniques can prove extremely helpful. As we become aware of our breathing we can influence the breathing of our horse, then tension levels can be lowered and more harmony maintained. We are encouraged by the medical profession to take up pursuits such as yoga or walking which help us to acquire a more relaxed rhythm in our breathing.

When we become stressed, one of the first symptoms is a change in breathing, which becomes more shallow and rapid. When this occurs, we may not be aware of it, unless we happen to be on stage and about to take part in a play or recite a poem; suddenly we can hardly breathe and it is difficult to formulate words or have any clarity of thought. This is a direct result of the increased heart rate.

If we can control our breathing, then we have more control over our body as a whole. Our responses, actions and thoughts can be more focused with maximum coordination. In this way we can connect with the mind of our horse, which in turn will help him to achieve his own harmony, settled energy and calmness. This may seem a very logical path of communication but, regretfully, one that we do not always seek to follow.

Control the breathing

When we learn to have more self-awareness, it will bring about changes in the way horses respond. Throughout this book we will be looking at the significance of the points made below.

- Our calmness and mood.
- Tuning in to our own breathing.

- An understanding of the importance of touch and gentle stroking.
- The significance of our personal body language to the horse.
- Our tone of voice.

Every person and each relationship is different and there are no rules for successful friendships or partnerships, only guidelines. All interaction becomes an exploration for each individual and our personalities change as we evolve throughout our lives. This book does not seek to give rules for relationships but hopefully to promote more insight into the ways of a horse working in tandem with human nature. Our communication skills lie in the art of understanding our own personalities as well as those of our horses.

Do any of the following make you think of anyone you know?

'She is so sensitive, you have to be really careful about choosing your words.'

'He is so impulsive; he just doesn't stop to think.'

'She just does not stop talking. She will never listen.'

'He is a total workaholic and just thrives on it.'

'She is so quiet you never quite know what she is thinking.'

'She has such a sense of humour and always manages to see the funny side of life.'

2.4 Relax and enjoy your horse

2.5 Cultivate a love for your horse

These few examples show that we all have our unique characteristics and we all respond in different ways with individual friends and members of our family. Every relationship will have the potential to encourage us to either develop and grow or to undermine our confidence and opinions. Do you treat everyone you meet identically? I doubt it. We may be very relaxed and open with certain people or wary of what we say to others. And so it is with our horses! (Figure 2.4.)

The art of horsemanship lies in understanding the personality of each horse as only then can we apply the subtlety of communications to gain the best response in training. We can gain all the technical knowledge available to us, but if we do not understand our horse, as an individual, very little will be gained. (Figure 2.5.)

Develop a love for your horse

This relationship between human and horse may take months of patience but the journey is one of empathy, not undertaken to please judges or spectators, but just for the love of the horse.

Levante enjoying his freedom (photo: Rafael Lemos)

Chapter Three

Loose Work

'In allowing a horse to be a horse we can become more effective as trainers'
Jenny Rolfe

We can all aspire to practise good horsemanship and the ability to listen to a horse is a basic requirement for achieving this goal. Loose work gives a trainer an opportunity to observe and listen to horses; the gifted horseman will understand that he should regard each horse as an individual and assess the path of training accordingly, building a relationship of trust and love. The time spent training from the ground helps to forge a partnership between horse and trainer, which will be invaluable when ridden work is commenced.

Our goal is to promote confidence between horse and handler in order to establish more harmony within the work. The horse will learn to relax and be more capable of working with loose and rhythmic gaits. We can either help him to grow in confidence or, through a lack of understanding, allow the horse to become a fearful and anxious pupil. It is therefore our responsibility to learn to communicate in a language the horse understands.

Training the Athlete

Talented human athletes can dedicate years to training, working towards a maximum fitness that could lead to competition prizes. They will either gain confidence, strength and ability in their chosen field or the pressure will cause them significant stress, which may affect their performance. Personalities alter with success and where some will dig deeply to find resources of great strength and courage, others will be overwhelmed by the pressure of achievement.

Horses can have the same diverse reactions to training and so we need to help them gain assurance and trust in their teacher. We should encourage the horse to have confidence in his own ability, which will assist his athletic development and progress. Our aim is not only to improve a gait or way of going but also to improve a relationship. Great athletes have to be on top form physically and their mental attitude has to be positive and confident. No athlete, whether human or equine, can give of their best if they are without self-confidence and are not correctly mentally prepared.

Loose Work as a Foundation

Loose work is a good foundation on which to construct the equine athlete's training. It enables us to communicate using body language, voice tone and breathing. Young horses can demonstrate their natural gaits at liberty but loose work will continue to be of value throughout a horse's training (Figure 3.1).

Loose work also has an important place in the re-education of a horse who has suffered a traumatic history. Horses taken beyond their limits mentally or physically will begin to respond in a positive way to loose work. They will be able to express a sense of their own freedom, whilst beginning to interact again with people. The horse is totally unrestricted by any tack or rider; hence all communication is **mind to mind**.

Allow the horse to be a horse

My Spanish Pure-bred stallion, Delfin, has been my greatest teacher. He thoroughly enjoys working loose, maybe as a result of past trauma endured as a bullfighting horse. Some horses

3.1 Joy in movement

appear to cope with this pressure but when I first saw Delfin he was highly anxious in body and mind. I had never ridden a horse with so much nervous, quivering energy and apprehension. Now, several years on, during our loose work in the school, he will watch me from maybe 20 m (66 ft) away. If I begin to walk laterally, he will follow my body language and perform a half-pass across the school. Delfin constantly observes my movements and will turn left or right and change from one gait to another mirroring my body language. He will follow me everywhere, as if on a lead, but the only contact is mind with mind. Delfin has sought this relationship and his supremely sensitive and intelligent mind enjoys this empathy in our communication. We have over the years worked together to change his traumatized personality into a more confident, rather extrovert stallion who loves people and himself!

The Objectives of Loose Work

- This initial education with a young horse can help to establish a relationship of trust where the horse will begin to look to his handler

Observe the mood of the horse

as the herd leader. This is an introduction for the horse to learn to work/play and interact with his handler.

- Loose work provides an opportunity to listen to and learn the language of the horse, using the power of breathing, body language and tone of voice.
- It is a time to observe the mood of the horse and develop further understanding of his personality.
- It is a time to observe the movement of the horse and detect any problems of stiffness or tension. It is interesting to see how the horse moves without weight on his back and whether he is a horse with a natural athletic ability.
- It gives an opportunity to the horse, without pressure, to develop a natural rhythm in his gaits without his balance being disturbed by the weight of a rider.
- The natural head carriage can be observed to see if the horse can stretch forward and lower his neck carriage naturally, or whether this might be difficult for him.
- The gaits can be assessed as can the natural balance within each gait.
- Trotting poles and jumping may be introduced. How the horse responds to new work, whether he is bold in nature or a little nervous, whether or not he will enjoy jumping and either his pleasure or lack of enthusiasm can all be noted. (Figure 3.2.)

3.2 Tinks stretches long and low over the trotting poles

- Signs of tension or relaxation can be observed by looking at the movement of the ears and tightness of the mouth and jaw and by assessing if the neck is tight and stiff or if the horse naturally moves with fluidity through his whole spine. A clamped, tight tail is a sign of tension; it should be slightly elevated and flowing.

Loose-schooling Techniques

A well-fenced arena, an indoor school or a round pen are the preferred areas in which to carry out the loose schooling. Here we can assess a young horse's mood and, if he is energetic, he will be able to demonstrate his exuberance safely. Even when training the more mature ridden horse, it is favourable to prepare with loose work so that he may loosen up muscles without the weight or restriction of the rider. A horse with too much excess energy who finds it difficult to settle down can release his excess tension whilst working loose. We want to achieve a calm, forward-going horse without confrontation, which is not always possible, but loose schooling will certainly help.

Imagine a 20 m x 40 m arena divided into two. Ideally two handlers will stand on the centre line of the arena, each about 10 m (33 ft) from either short side. Each handler will be responsible for encouraging the horse forward at their end of the arena. On the left rein, the whip is held in the right hand and the handler will adopt a position as if lungeing. He should place his body so that his right shoulder is aligned to direct his body energy towards the area of the horse that lies just behind the shoulder. The energy is an invisible line from your right shoulder and core stability directed towards the horse, encouraging him away and forwards. If you have a ball in your hand and position yourself to throw the ball underhand, this is a similar 'body energy' to that you should direct towards the horse. The horse instinctively moves away from the body language. The handler uses the whip to maintain the impulsion by following the horse's quarters with it. The whip can be trailed loosely along the ground if the horse is moving with sufficient energy but if he is not, it should be lightly cracked behind him and he should be encouraged with the voice. (Figures 3.3a and b.)

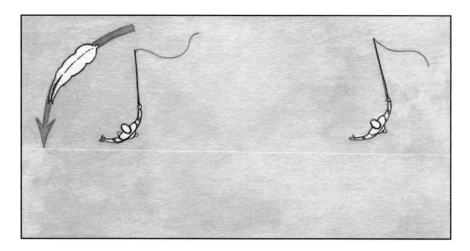

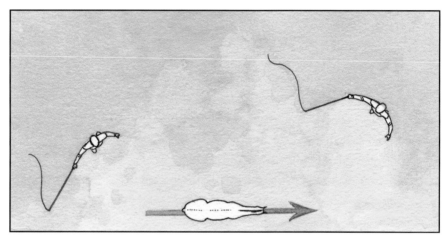

3.3a and b Loose work with two handlers

The horse is guided around one half of the arena towards the other handler who uses his body and whip position to keep the horse moving forward and around his short side of the school and on down the long side again.

A lazy horse should be encouraged to show some energy; an energetic horse should be loose schooled until he finds a steady rhythm and begins to relax. The horse will soon adapt from using the whole school to circling around one of the handlers as if on the lunge. The horse is encouraged to move forward by both the handlers. If a handler directs the horse around the short end of the school and continues to move on a small circle, the horse will learn to respond to the handler's position, which directs him to work on a circle as if he were being lunged, but with no lungeing equipment. The first handler uses the whip to stop the horse from working down the long side and the second handler encourages the horse to continue working on a circle around him (Figure 3.4). Verbal directions can be given: w-a-l-k, t-rot, and can-ter.

3.4 The first handler blocks the horse's path whilst the second handler encourages the horse to work on the circle

We can progress quickly to using breathing only. The trainer uses the outward breath to instigate an upward transition and the deeper inward breath for the downward transition. If the horse does not respond to these breathing techniques together with the body language, the voice and whip can be use to re-enforce the command. The trainer's breathing changes his body stance. For example, the deep inward breath strengthens and lengthens the spine and the horse quickly observes this change in posture. The deep outward breath relaxes and directs energy away from the trainer, towards the horse, who will recognize this body language as being the same as that of the herd. I must add that many horses are extremely perceptive and tune in extremely quickly to the techniques of breathing.

After a period of time the handler will notice that the horse starts to lick his lips, lower his head and neck and attempts to slow the pace. The inside ear flicks back and the horse is saying, 'I am ready to listen to you'. (The response time varies with each horse: a more dominant horse may take longer to respond, as will a more energetic horse.) When you notice these responses slow your walk and take a deep breath inwards. Lower the whip and turn your body slowly inwards facing the centre of your circle. You will then find that the horse will stop and turn inwards to face your back. When you approach the horse (either backwards or by turning to face him), walk with a lowered head and relaxed shoulders, keeping your whip softly lowered in your hand. The posture should be relaxed and inviting. The horse should be encouraged to stay on the circle and not to walk into the centre to the handler as this may cause problems later on in lungeing. If the horse starts to walk in, use assertive body language by moving towards him to encourage him to maintain his position on the circle.

At every stage of teaching, from basic to more advanced work, we will continue to use these techniques to re-establish the relationship between horse and trainer. If he listens to you and of his own freewill responds to your commands, your relationship is ready to be taken a step further.

Throughout the loose schooling, the horse will be constantly giving us signals, showing us whether he is in accord with our thoughts, or distracted and ignoring our directions. If he is listening, he will be relaxed in the neck and back but if he is inattentive he will be rushing around with his head in the air or may even be bucking. When he begins to accept the instruction, his inside ear starts to come back. Loose schooling is about being of one mind with a horse and if our thought process can

Communicate
mind to mind

build an empathy with the horse, the ridden work will take these communication skills even further.

When the horse is moving away at our request with his inside ear flicking backwards and forwards with an expression of concentration we know we are connected with his mind. If he raises his head because something distracts him, we need to quickly reinforce our authority with our body language, voice and breathing.

Over a period of time a horse will understand that when we work together we want him to be responsive to our commands and that nothing else is important. We need to teach him to focus, relax and work with calmness and energy.

Building an Awareness of Body Language in Loose Schooling

Our body language can give many mixed messages to a horse. If we walk into a stable or school hastily, marching towards the horse with an arrogant stance, he will immediately feel tense and threatened. If we want to work with a calm horse, who wishes to interact with us, then we need to be 'body aware' from the moment we enter the area. When we walk steadily and calmly, breathing in a relaxed way, the horse will sense our mood and respond with a more confident attitude. This assurance will be transmitted from us to him and is the bond to be cultivated throughout his training. If you relax the shoulders and lower the stance of your body, your horse will not feel intimidated. In addition, the voice and touch should be gentle and kind; the horse responds contentedly to the more gentle touch.

Become aware of your body language

There will certainly be times when the horse requires discipline and then more assertive body language and a dominant tone of voice must be used quickly to re-establish leadership. We need to be consistent in our actions because this is the way the horse learns when we are pleased and when we will not tolerate misbehaviour.

The body language used in loose work is focused towards pushing the horse away and directing the handler's energy towards the area behind his shoulder. I believe the horse is responsive to body language because of his natural instinct to move away from any threat. In the wild, a predator will always attack an equine in its most vulnerable area just behind the withers. The horse cannot easily reach this area to bite or kick in self-defence. Consequently, it is incredible that horses actually allow humans (potential predators) to sit in this vulnerable area.

If, therefore, he feels our body language is directed in this manner, he will naturally move away. I do not believe that this training makes him fearful but the instinct to move away from, and not confront, a threat remains deep within him. (Figures 3.5a and b.)

Advancing Your Skills: Loose Work with One Handler

Once the horse has become accustomed to loose work with two handlers and understands change of gait and direction, it should be possible to work the horse with just one handler, which is similar to lungeing on a circle but

3.5a and b a) By directing your body language you can encourage a horse to move away, and b) Delfin responds to the language of the herd communicating with body language and breathing rather than lungeing equipment. Some horses appear to enjoy this work more than others, however the speed of response will vary from horse to horse. The horse can be taught to listen to your voice commands initially but, as he learns to recognize a pattern of breathing with each command, he will quickly respond just to this. Horses become anxious when given heavy strong aids but appear to react instinctively to breathing only. These techniques are discussed in more detail in Chapter 7 so that the methods can be more easily understood by the handler.

The breathing techniques I use have evolved slowly, with time spent trying them on horses of different breeds. I have found the understanding of breathing awareness to be very helpful in dealing with horses suffering from stress. Young horses brought in straight from the herd also appear to be very responsive to these techniques; perhaps they are looking for familiar signs, similar to those experienced within the herd.

Stand in the centre of the school, with your whip in your right hand and your horse moving on the left rein. Take a deep breath inwards and then, at the same moment as you breathe out deeply, move your body towards the horse.

Your right shoulder should be directed behind the inside shoulder of the horse. As you take a step towards the horse and use the outward breath and voice command, the horse should walk forward. The whip is positioned to follow the horse. To maintain the circle you will need to keep him moving forward by angling your body position towards his shoulder backed up by the voice and whip if necessary.

After several walk strides you can ask the horse to move forwards into trot, by taking a deep breath inwards. On the strong outward breath give the 't-rot' command and encourage him forward with your body positioned, and walking assertively, towards him and backed up with the whip, if necessary. It usually only requires this to be repeated a few times for the outward breath alone to trigger the upward transitions.

Once the horse is trotting forwards on the circle, maintain your position, until you want him to walk. Then, slow your walk and take a deep breath inwards. This deep inhalation will rebalance and strengthen your body position; the horse will learn to copy your body language and come back down into walk.

When you want the horse to change direction, bring him down to walk. If you are walking on the left rein, you will be directing his movement with your right-hand side and the whip held in your right hand. Slowly change the whip from the right to the left hand by passing it behind your body. Proceed to walk more quickly until parallel with the horse's shoulder.

Now turn towards the horse bringing your left shoulder around and proceed to walk on the right rein, encouraging the horse with your left shoulder and body directed towards him (Figures 3.6a, b and c).

3.6a, b and c a) Turn towards your horse bringing your left shoulder around; b) Instigate the change of direction with your left shoulder and body; c) Continue to bring your left shoulder around and proceed to walk forwards

a

b

c

Remember that directing your 'body energy' is similar to throwing a ball underhand; allow the motion of energy to move towards the horse's inside shoulder. If necessary, the left hand and the whip are directed behind the horse to encourage forward movement.

Use your body energy directed towards the horse with a deep outward breath to move into trot; again, re-enforcing the instruction with the whip and voice if necessary (Figures 3.6d, e and f).

d

3.6d, e and f d) Direct your energy towards the horse; e) Use your outward breath and body energy to move the horse into trot; f) The horse has responded by moving into an energetic trot

e

f

Here Delfin works correctly through a change of direction to the left (Figures 3.7a, b and c).

3.7a, b and c a) Delfin becomes a mirror of Jenny's body language and begins to change direction; b) Delfin continues to change direction; c) Delfin moves off in the new direction still aware of Jenny's breathing and body language

When you finish the lesson, turn away from him, in towards the centre of the circle, relax your shoulders and your posture and he should come to a halt, facing towards you. If working on the left rein, you turn away from him, drawing your right shoulder into the centre of the circle. When lungeing, you use different body language so that when he halts he remains on the circle and does not turn in.

This awareness of breathing and rebalancing in body and mind is also the essence of the ridden half-halt which is described more fully later in this book.

It is important to be patient with both yourself and your horse. It is possible to learn this system of communication with no previous experience and allow your horse to be your teacher. Observe his responses to your body language, there is much to learn and enjoy.

Loose Jumping

Jumps for gymnastic work can also be placed down the long side of the school and, on command, the horse can enjoy loose jumping as part of his training (Figure 3.8). The importance of this exercise is to teach the horse to use himself more athletically. It is not, therefore, necessary for him to jump high fences; small jumps carefully spaced in gymnastic grids are more suitable. The jumps can be placed with either one stride between them or with a bounce stride in and out. The grids teach the horse to think for himself, to evaluate his take-off and landing between related distances, and to judge height, distance and the best place to take off before a fence. Most horses take great pleasure in this type of loose work.

This is a time to enjoy the communication with your horse and allow him to learn an energetic way of going, combined with a relaxed and happy attitude. The body language is the same as that used for loose

3.8 Maestu enjoying his loose jumping

ground work with two handlers but now jumps are added down the long side of the school.

I will expound on the value of loose work further by introducing two Spanish stallions, both presenting different problems. I have chosen to use loose work as a holistic approach to establish the cause of complex behaviour problems and to re-evaluate the relationship between human and horse.

Case Study 1:
Generoso, Spanish Pure-bred Stallion

Generoso is a beautiful Spanish Pure-bred stallion. If we look at his traumatic experiences it may help to define the significance of loose schooling.

His story begins on a magnificent 500 acre estate, nestling along the banks of the river Blackwater near Youghal in Southern Ireland. Several years ago Helen imported Generoso from Spain and we began having regular discussions about stallion behaviour on the telephone. Over a period of time I realized that Generoso was causing Helen some considerable anguish.

A groom had been employed to look after Helen's horses because she was unable to ride after sustaining a fall. She had begun to lose touch with the situation building up in the stable yard between her stallion and groom; he had become terrified of the horse and things deteriorated rapidly. Generoso began to sense his fear and started to launch himself at, and attack, the groom. Eventually there was a dreadful incident when the groom, whilst shouting and waving his whip around caused Generoso to rear up and as he came down his hooves caught Helen. As a result she received several injuries.

Over a period of time Helen employed further grooms and trainers but, although gentle and kind at times, Generoso would continue to show aggression.

After several telephone conversations with Helen, I could not resist her invitation to Ireland to attempt to find solutions to the problems being, by then, experienced on a daily basis. On arrival at the magnificent stable yard I was introduced to the stallion and immediately saw his menacing aggressive attitude. He was saying to me, in the only language he understood, 'Keep out of my space – I do not trust you'. I spent a sleepless night considering how to turn this situation around.

Several years of my life had been spent fostering teenagers with major behavioural problems and seeking reasons for their behaviour patterns while looking for a positive way forward. Frequently, aggressive behaviour stemmed from abuse, lack of trust in adults and little hope of any love from the parents. All of the children were missing a role model whom they could love and trust. Maybe Generoso was having problems with his identity and was in need of a herd leader, a role model to respect. Once he could gain trust in a herd leader then his own confidence could grow. Hopefully his need for aggression would cease as he could begin to feel more calm and secure.

Security is gained from instruction

The following morning I asked if Generoso could be taken to the indoor school, where I could work with him from the ground. This brought a small group of spectators to the school who were intrigued to see how I fared as most of them were nervous of him loose in the stable.

Generoso and I stood looking at each other in the school and then I proceeded with body language and whip to encourage him to trot and canter in a circle around me. Even when he showed signs of lowering his head with his inside ear back I continued working him forward. Then I lowered my stance and turned away from him looking inwards and he halted turning to face me. I walked backward slowly towards him and talked softly until I was directly in front of him. With cues from my body position and the whip, he changed direction and continued working in trot and canter until he was prepared to work with me on the new rein. After the change of direction, it took a little while before he responded as well.

I then led Generoso back to the stable and felt that he was beginning to acknowledge me as his herd leader. Previously he was menacing to lead in hand as he would lunge at the handler but now, after the loose work, I felt a more submissive response.

We repeated the same work over several days, until I felt that he was really listening to me and demonstrating respect for my commands. Our bond was increasing with trust and empathy gained from the loose work, so we decided he was ready for further instruction, under saddle.

3.9 Beginning a new relationship based on leadership and trust

When I began to ride him, I found Generoso to be a highly trained horse, with great sensitivity and he was a joy to ride. His attitude towards me as a rider was cooperative as a result of the bond established through the groundwork. A feeling of confidence and trust were slowly beginning to replace his insecurity.

I was relieved to leave Helen with the beginnings of a new relationship with Generoso, based on a deeper understanding of his nature (Figure 3.9).

I asked Helen to assess what she had learnt from my visit and her thoughts were expressed thus: 'Humans look for love and affection to gain their confidence and try to direct this towards the horse. The horse however understands leadership and respect; his confidence is gained through this'. She added, 'I am now giving Generoso directions and he gives back affection with no fear. He seems to gain security through my instruction. My confidence has grown as I am more aware of the relationship he seeks'.

> The confidence of the horse is gained from leadership and respect

The importance of the loose work to establish firm relationships cannot be over-emphasized. All our young mares and stallions regularly participate in this type of work. I used to be keen to start the work under saddle, but having seen the benefits of the loose work with many horses I think the time spent on the ground can prove invaluable as a tool of communication.

Case Study 2: Maromo, Spanish Pure-bred Stallion

I first saw Maromo in Spain and he certainly impressed me with his superb gaits and beauty. He was ridden in draw reins, which I thought was slightly unusual as his conformation was good and these extra gadgets should not have been necessary.

Eventually Maromo was sold to an aspiring dressage rider in England who saw his potential and was looking forward to competing with him in the future.

When he arrived in England it seemed that some progress was being made in his training but over a period of time Maromo became reluctant to go forward and would twist his head and neck upwards and to the left when ridden. His owner, Gillian, phoned me several times to say that Maromo was not willing to work and seemed very agitated. She was unsure whether the arrival of a new stallion next door had caused him stress or if he had suffered any previous injury either in the field or the stable. Gillian sought to give him a varied work programme including loose work, lungeing and training under saddle.

I was asked to assess the situation, after several months of deterioration. Initially the deterioration was seen in the general performance of the horse but rapidly involved the whole relationship between rider and horse. Both were frustrated and anxious about any ridden work. When Maromo eventually came to our yard for assessment and training he had not been ridden for a couple of months. Gillian had felt that he was so unhappy about being ridden that she only asked him to work on the lunge. He had appeared content to be lunged but under saddle he was so tense that his back went up and he said 'no' whenever he was asked to go forward into trot.

A mutual friend, who was an experienced rider, had also attempted to ride Maromo, but she said that he felt very tense and dangerous with a totally rigid back, so she decided to dismount!

There was much for me to think about as similar symptoms can be produced by a challenging horse who is lacking discipline and respect. The horse will be taking the dominant role and will challenge more fiercely for the right to do things his way. I had to take a good long look at Maromo's nature and decide whether he was at this stage or whether stress or physical discomfort was causing the problem.

During my nursing years, my patients could normally communicate with ease, telling me about their aches and pains. Horses can only give us signals through their behaviour when all is not well, and so it becomes our responsibility to take a step back and observe the horse closely to try to read correctly the signs he is giving us.

Maromo came to stay with us for several weeks so that I could have the opportunity to assess the cause of his behaviour. On his arrival in our yard, Maromo was very anxious and stressed; before any progress could be made, therefore, we had to give him the opportunity to relax. His eyes showed anxiety and he was unable to stand calmly in the stable.

Our first lesson together was in the school. I was about to commence lungeing when suddenly, without any indication from me, he flew off, rushing round and round. Slowly I brought him back to halt and realized that initially it was most important that he learnt to stand calmly, with me, before we started any further training. Consequently, I stood with him, just stroking his neck and face and breathing and sighing deeply, searching for some response. He needed to feel that he could be calm and begin to trust me. During all our work together, we would stop every few minutes to help him release any built-up tension. He slowly learnt to breathe more deeply and you could hear him blow gently through his nostrils in relaxation. Sometimes it would be a much deeper sigh of contentment. I encourage all horses to do this at times during training and at the end of a work session. If I use my own breathing pattern and take a very deep long sigh, the horse will frequently copy this, which helps to release tension.

I spent time grooming and stroking him to see if there were any particularly sensitive areas of his body which might indicate a physical problem. The healed wound from an old injury was still quite sensitive. After any major wound, the new tissue growth will often be more sensitive, depending on the regeneration of the nerve endings in the area.

The following weeks were spent building a more trusting relationship and calming down Maromo's anxious mind. I found him to have a generous and highly sensitive nature which always wanted to please. He lacked confidence in his own identity, and so it now seemed unlikely that the cause of the problem was an arrogant nature but, increasingly, it appeared that his anxiety was quite deep-rooted. Depressed horses just stare ahead, almost blindly, and become sullen and introverted, very nearly giving up on life. Anxious horses fidget constantly and their eyes dart around without purpose. Their necks and bodies are tense, and their gaits are rushed and stilted. They do not listen to you as their minds are somewhere else. Sadly for many horses, this is the time they are punished for evasion which only increases the struggle for harmonious communication.

After several weeks with Maromo, I noticed a change in his behaviour as he became more relaxed in the stable and calm in the school. He would stand quietly before loose schooling and then walk and trot in a loose and balanced way around the school. I always took my time with him, no rushing, just calm and patient handling. I soon decided that he was more secure in his mind and ready for some ridden work. I started by riding him in walk for several minutes. At first I felt his back tighten but I continued quietly and he responded. I paid attention to his breathing and encouraged the outward sigh each time we halted.

The trot work was interesting as previously he had challenged the rider and refused to move forward. When we began trot, I asked for walk again after only a few strides whilst quietly stroking his neck. I wanted him to think that it was easy just to trot for a short distance. This method appeared to work, as within days he would work in walk and trot in a more relaxed manner. After several sessions under saddle, I came to the conclusion that, although Maromo was calmer, he was still presenting some physical problems.

Following a discussion with his breeder, I found out that Maromo's scar was the result of a serious injury he sustained as a youngster. The assessment I made after our time together was that Maromo required further investigation from an experienced cranial osteopath. I have found that cranial treatment is a very good, sensitive way to reveal deep-rooted trauma, sometimes suffered many years ago. His treatment confirmed my intuition and observations, as the cranial osteopath found problems related to both physical trauma and emotional stress.

It is very difficult to understand some of the complex behaviour in our horses and we will never be correct every time in our assessments. However, by observation and with patience, we can certainly learn a great deal as we seek to listen to, explore and communicate in their language.

Maestu jumping on the lunge

Chapter Four

Lungeing

A logical system of work, clearly understood by both rider and horse, is fundamental to any progress whether we are training a youngster or re-educating an older horse. Our communication developed in loose schooling can be taken a stage further in the work on the lunge. The horse should already be responsive to our voice commands, breathing and body language and should be well prepared to progress with this next phase of learning.

Lungeing will enable us to teach the horse good foundations for his future ridden work. He will be building the necessary muscle structure to prepare him to receive the weight of a rider on his back and is given this opportunity to work in his normal balance before he has to carry a rider, who will disturb his natural self-carriage.

An older horse may also benefit from lungeing if he has been out of training for a while and is being brought back into ridden work. It can be useful to lunge a horse when he has previously sustained an injury that has prevented him from having regular exercise. Lunge work could be beneficial to a mare if she has had a long time off work because of pregnancy and rearing a foal.

Lungeing on the circle may not be suitable in all circumstances, after trauma, for example, when the concentrated circle work may be too stressful. It is advisable to discuss the history of any accident with a veterinary surgeon or a physiotherapist before commencing this type of fitness training.

Lungeing Equipment

The following equipment can be used for lungeing.
- A snaffle bridle with reins twisted and looped through the throatlash.
- A roller (with padding to protect the withers and spine) or saddle.
- Side reins.
- Cavesson or *serreta*. (The Spanish or Portuguese *serreta* is a metal, noseband that is fitted to lie in the same position as a drop noseband. It should be extremely well padded and covered in leather to protect the horse's nose. It is an instrument of great control in subtle hands but in the wrong hands it can do great damage and should never be used by the inexperienced. For training it can be used like a cavesson to take a lunge rein and, when the horse graduates to a bit, can be left on the bridle as an extra means of control. Stallions being led or shown in hand will usually wear a *serreta*.) I would advocate the use of the smooth, not the toothed, *serreta*, preferably covered with leather and sheepskin over the top, and I would not normally use it for ridden work.
- Lunge line (rein).
- Lunge whip.
- Exercise boots for foreleg protection.

Thoughts on Lungeing

I lunge on circles of varying diameters depending upon the type of work and stage of development of the horse. A lengthening of the outside of the horse and a relaxation of the inside of his outline should be encouraged, following the line of the circle.

I begin by working on a circle of about 15 m but if the horse is too energetic and rushes, it is helpful to encourage him onto a smaller circle. He then has to steady his speed to maintain his balance, and by using our body language and a soft voice tone, we can influence him more easily. The horse can be made more attentive by a quick jerk or vibration of the wrist on the lunge line. When he is obedient, relax the pressure on the line so that he does not become heavy on the lunge line and pulls on it.

The inside hind leg of the horse takes more weight on the circle and the changes of direction will help to create suppleness. Every horse is stiffer on one side and more flexible on the other. Initially, during the first months of training, the horse may appear more crooked or stiff on one rein. Correct lungeing, should create more suppleness and freedom of movement for the horse in both directions and this should be one of our training goals. We need to take this into consideration during our work and not demand too much of the horse by excess work on his stiffer side. I have noticed that the response to commands can vary from one rein to another. A lesson or command taught on one rein may cause him some confusion when he changes direction. He is not being awkward; it is just that the learning process for him may vary from one rein to the other. Humans are dominant with either the right or the left side and we must also allow for this trait in the horse during training.

If a horse is fidgety and uncomfortable at any time during the lunge work, it may be that after working in side reins (see page 95) for a time, his neck is a little stiff and sore. Should this happen I will remove the side reins and just walk him for a few moments before continuing with the lesson. If he stretches his neck downwards and forwards when the side reins are removed, then he is seeking to stretch the muscles he has been using, which is a good sign. It is important for a horse to have short periods of relaxation and to encourage him to stretch the neck forwards and down; this, in turn, will lengthen, stretch and relax all the muscles along the top line which have been working hard.

It is essential during the early stages of training that the young horse

Make frequent changes of direction

Encourage fluid and energetic gaits

Learn the
importance
of timing:
when to
finish a
lesson

has short breaks from constant pressure, when developing both his concentration and physical ability. Overwork for long periods of time can produce sour and uncooperative horses. Consideration is needed for his stage of development and fitness, both mentally and physically. Remember, we need to be constantly aware of the messages and signals we receive from the horse's body language.

The timing of a lesson is of the utmost importance. If we can finish a lesson on a really good note, a horse can return to his stable without feeling overworked or stressed and will be content to work the following day. A horse taught in this way will be able to progress with his training, working with calmness and empathy with his handler.

The horse should be encouraged to feel relaxed in his work, yet also be focused and energetic. It will not help his training if his natural instinct of fear and flight is continuously provoked by anger or impatience, which will make the horse rigid with tension causing him to tighten his neck and his back. His gaits will become stilted and he will stick his head in the air, aware of everything but his handler. This behaviour will not give us a chance to encourage him to learn. Fear and flight means just that; a horse has to react with speed, to run away from a predator and he cannot learn once these strong instincts for survival have come to the forefront of his mind.

As stated, we are looking for attentiveness from the horse, with a lowered head and relaxed neck carriage, and so we need to cultivate a calm and willing attitude. When the horse gives us his confidence, he will relax at the poll more willingly and take a contact with the bit. We cannot force the horse to come on the bit correctly; initially the horse has to feel mentally relaxed which will then bring about the physical relaxation needed for correct contact. Tight side reins whilst lungeing or a restricted contact in ridden work have nothing to do with a horse working in self-carriage; he is simply responding with tension to a feeling of restriction. Tightness is tension. Relaxation in balance with energy and submission is the path to true self-carriage.

It is important to show a horse that the lunge whip is not an instrument of punishment; he needs to have respect for the whip but not be scared of it. His acceptance of the whip should be cultivated by stroking him gently along his neck and back and touching his legs with it. The onus is on us to build up the horse's positive attitude to his training by the way we use the whip. It is simply a tool of encouragement that helps us gain his concentration and impulsion but it can *only* be an effective tool to reinforce our leadership if used with respect, wisdom and good timing. If we use the whip simultaneously with the vocal aids given in encouraging, and not aggressive, tones, the horse will learn to accept the whip without fear.

Benefits of Lungeing

- Lungeing provides an opportunity to introduce the young horse to the bridle, roller or saddle and side reins.
- It prepares the horse to receive a rider with confidence and security.
- It teaches the horse to accept instruction and to understand the trainer's voice together with his breathing and body language.
- Lungeing teaches the horse to work on circles with rhythm, cadence and balance (self-carriage) in the gaits (Figure 4.1).

4.1 Maestu working with rhythm, cadence and balance in self-carriage

- It helps the horse to learn how to move in balance and self-carriage and to develop correct muscle structure, which ensures the horse is well prepared to receive the weight of a rider on his back.
- It is a method of warming-up before any ridden work or schooling.
- It provides an opportunity to observe the horse from the ground, his mood for the day and his gaits.
- The trainer can assess the horse whilst lungeing, which may influence the type of work continued under saddle.

Lungeing the Young Horse

A young horse should be introduced to every new stage of training very slowly with care and confidence. Initially he will need to become accustomed to the snaffle bridle and a roller before lungeing is attempted. Time, patience and correct handling will ensure that the horse accepts new instructions with trust. It will be helpful to have two handlers initially until the horse has a better understanding of what is required of him.

Introduce the lungeing tack to the horse whilst he is in his stable, his place of security. At first, the roller should be placed just lightly on his back and when he accepts this it can be done up, but not too tightly. Meanwhile, the horse should be encouraged just to stand calmly. If at any stage he becomes agitated, use a soothing voice, relaxed breathing and body language to reduce tension. Stroke his neck gently and walk around him reassuring him all the time. I think that horses prefer soft stroking to strong patting; stroking can help them to feel calmer. Allow the horse just to stand and gain confidence with the new weight on his back before asking him to walk around in it.

The same principles should be applied to introducing the bit. Never

Patience produces confidence

do this in a hurry, as he will sense any impatience and probably throw his head about to avoid the bit. It is best to use titbits and slowly encourage his head downwards, towards the bit. Sometimes I remove the bit from the bridle and just put it in his mouth, maybe with a handful of nuts, to let him chew and play with it.

When introducing new lessons it is very important to keep everything steady and calm. If you meet resistance, try to go back to the stage when the horse was last calm. The day will come when you feel that he is ready to have all the tack put on and to be walked out of the stable. If you have worked well with the horse and he has built up confidence in you, then this should progress well. If your plans begin to go wrong, however, there is always another day and so try to finish at a moment when things are going well, with the horse still feeling confident and assured.

Side Reins

Lunging without side reins
A lungeing session should start without the side reins being fitted. This gives the horse an opportunity to play a little and allows him to work without restriction (Figure 4.2). He can be allowed to express his exuberance as a confident, happy horse, full of health and vitality. Excess

4.2 Lungeing without side reins allows Kiri to find her balance and develop her gaits without restriction.

energy under saddle might cause confrontation between horse and rider and we are trying to work with the nature of the horse and not against it. However, if natural exuberance is taken too far, the handler should use soft tones to encourage the horse to calm and steady the pace; short vibrations on the lunge line using the wrist can also ask the horse to become more attentive.

When you are ready to begin lungeing, stand in the centre of the circle with a second handler (if the horse is inexperienced) positioned on the circle, to the outside of the horse. He can then reinforce any commands and also give the horse reassurance and guidance. Initially the horse should stand calmly before moving off into walk. Keep everything relaxed, this will encourage the horse to move off quietly instead of exploding into his gaits.

Throughout training re-establish the relationships of the herd

If a horse does not listen to your commands then there are ways of regaining authority; he must learn to respect the handler right from the start. We have different options with our communication but the horse has to learn that the trainer will be his leader. The aim is to establish a relationship in which the horse looks to this leader for direction but this takes time and patience. During the loose work a horse is taught to respect and listen to his herd leader and this relationship should be maintained throughout all aspects of training. I am always prepared to go back to this communication to re-establish these important herd relationships.

For example, when being lunged he may canter round the school ignoring all instructions to come back down into trot. Allow him to continue in canter but when he *offers* to come back into trot, encourage him to keep cantering; he will soon realize that it is the trainer who is instructing and that it is he who will instigate the transitions. Another tactic to calm a headstrong personality is to decrease the size of the canter circle, which will make it more difficult for him to balance. Then, bring him back down to trot, on a smaller circle and, after several strides, ask him to strike off in canter again, allowing the horse to work on a larger circle once more.

The handler should have the same contact with the lunge line as that with the reins when riding. Again, short vibrations from the wrist should be used on the lunge line to gain attention (Figure 4.3). When the horse is working correctly on the circle, the contact should be light, allowing the horse to experience lightness within his own balance. Every opportunity should be given by the handler to allow the horse his own self-carriage and not allow him to lean on a contact with the lunge line.

4.3 Short vibrations on the lunge line will gain attention

It may help to visualize a hexagonal figure rather than a circle (Figure 4.4). Every few strides, give a short vibration on the lunge line with the wrist to gain the horse's concentration and to indicate the direction in which he is to work. After a few strides ask the horse to make a slight turn, as though following the hexagonal shape; this re-establishes engagement of the inside hind and helps to keep the correct bend on the circle. The whip can then be used to encourage the hind limbs to step under the body and maintain impulsion. Ensure the body language is correct as the inside shoulder of the handler will need to follow the inside shoulder of the horse. If the

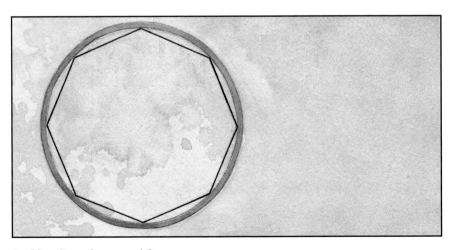

4.4 Visualize a hexagonal figure

handler maintains his position at the centre of the circle, this will encourage the horse to continue in a true circle around him. Only work on a true circle can develop true cadence.

The horse should settle into a more regular rhythmic trot before the side reins are introduced.

Introducing the side reins

The lunge line may be attached to the cavesson or the *serreta*, which is placed over the snaffle bridle. I lunge using the centre ring and attach the side reins, when appropriate, to the roller from the snaffle rings.

When putting side reins on a young horse for the first time I would normally only fit the outside rein, fairly loosely. When the horse begins to accept this rein and relaxes his neck into a contact (not away from it), we can then fit the inside rein. This process normally eliminates the resistance that two side reins can produce at first. The restriction can cause fear and the horse can express this by rearing up or leaping about to avoid the contact.

Side reins are for guidance, not restriction

Once the horse is ready for the second side rein, the outside rein should be about two holes longer than the inside rein to allow the horse to stretch through his top line when working on a circle.

If you are unsure of the correct length for the side reins, offer the horse a titbit from your hand and use it to encourage him to arch his neck up and out away from the withers and to relax and lower his head from the poll area. The head should be in front of the vertical and the side reins should be long enough to accept this outline (Figures 4.5a and b). At first, I usually make the side reins a couple of holes longer to encourage the horse to work into the contact without feeling too restricted. If the side reins are not allowing sufficient lengthening of the neck and the horse looks tense and taut, then bring him back to halt and lengthen the reins.

When a horse takes a step forward from halt, the first part of his body to move is his head and neck. We must, therefore, ensure he is comfortable in his movement. A feeling of restriction may suppress his desire to move forwards with enthusiasm and confidence.

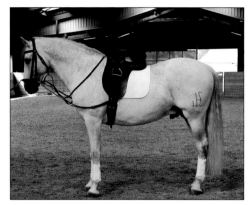

4.5a and b a) Fitting side reins to a roller over the saddle; b) Fitting side reins directly to the saddle

A young horse may have natural athletic ability but his muscle tone will need to be improved and the introduction of side reins will help to build the correct musculature. Young horses require longer side reins while this is being developed but they can be shortened as the training progresses and the muscles are built up. The basic training is designed to encourage correct development of the muscles, which will support the horse when he carries a rider. The horse's mind is also being stimulated on a path of education, preparing him well for the ridden work.

The horse should work actively from behind into an energetic but loose frame with the neck stretching up and out from the withers. This should encourage a lengthening of the top line. The lower muscles of the neck should always be soft and relaxed, never restricted or tight.

> The whip should be used to encourage and motivate

The trainer should employ the same techniques of breathing, body position and voice in lungeing as are used in loose work, with the whip being used to gain impulsion.

Lungeing Problems

Emphasis must be placed on teaching a horse to halt calmly and await instruction. Some horses are so anxious to get going that this small, but important, lesson is overlooked and it can become a problem. The first moments of a lunge session should always be spent calmly at halt before work commences and, no matter how forward-thinking the horse is, he must wait for the command to move off. It is good to spend a little time in walk so that the horse will understand transitions from walk to trot, rather than commencing the lunge session by rushing straight into trot work. This is the work ethic to be encouraged when the horse is under saddle, and so we should begin to teach him good habits in this early stage of training.

Transitions from walk to trot and trot to walk will help us to lay the foundations for more submission, obedience and collection during the training.

If a horse is rather lazy by nature, we can decrease the size of the lungeing circle to maybe 10 m or 12 m. This will enable the trainer to be more effective with his body position and lunge whip to stimulate more vigorous forward movement.

Should the horse turn in to face you when you are lungeing on your own without an assistant, encourage him forward again on the circle immediately. If a command for a transition from trot to walk is ignored, vibrate the lunge line to gain his attention. In addition, take a deep breathe inwards, slow down your own walk and use a calm tone of voice. If he continues to ignore commands, then choose a point on the circle, well in front of the path of the horse. Walk towards this point to block his path; this body language together with the verbal instruction given in a slow, steady tone should bring him down to walk. The horse will learn to respond to the voice aid alone very quickly.

You want the horse to track on a true circle and if the horse tries to cut in from this, then we use our body language to encourage him back into the larger circle. This should be done by taking a positive step forwards towards his shoulder with an assertive voice command. The horse learns through repetition and often, in the same part of the circle, he will slow down, fall in off the circle or attempt to swing his quarters away. This frequently happens in the middle of the school, rather than in the corners.

The trainer must keep one step ahead and anticipate these responses. If the horse continually swings his quarters out when he arrives near the centre line, there are methods to counteract the problem. If the horse is trotting, one technique that works well is to ask for walk well before the normal place of evasion. Maintain the walk for several strides and just before the centre line, ask for trot again. The horse will often step forward on the correct circle because his original thought pattern has been changed and replaced with an acknowledgement of your commands. This is the art of communicating: understanding the horse and putting your thoughts into his mind. In this way, he will become your mirror and finest teacher.

If the horse asserts his strength on the lunge, short and, possibly, strong actions of the wrist and hand are required to command his attention. Positive deeper breathing will give the handler better posture and more core stability, and the horse will find it more difficult to resist the stronger body position. If the horse continues to dominate, he should be brought on to a smaller circle as he will have to steady his pace to retain his balance. Once the submissive connection is restored, the tension in the lunge line can be relaxed. You can slow your body language and use your voice tone to steady him. I sometimes lunge using a corner of the school which helps to concentrate the horse's mind and prevents him from trying to pull away. The wall can be used to guide him onto the circle required. The horse should be encouraged to maintain a good circle progressing with steady, rhythmic and energetic strides.

If the horse is not working in a balanced outline, i.e. leaning too much weight on the inside shoulder and looking outwards, he needs to be brought back on to a small circle again. A lack of engagement of the inside hind leg can induce this lack of submission to the circle.

Touching his inside leg with the whip and using your body position towards his shoulder should motivate him to move away. At the same time use your body position and a quick vibration of the lunge line with the wrist to ask for more attention and the correct neck flexion.

You can guide the horse to flex correctly and lower his neck in the direction of the circle. As he begins to work correctly, relax the contact on the lunge line; it is important for the horse to learn how to move properly in self-carriage and not to lean on the lunge. The lunge line gives directional and positional guidance.

When the horse is working submissively to the curve of the circle, the diameter of the circle can then be increased again.

Exercises in Balance for the Trainer

Trainers can increase their awareness of balance and self-carriage by trying a few exercises without the horse. Place your hands on your hips and walk a 10 m (33ft) circle. Note the larger swing of the outside hip and leg required to pivot your body-weight around the circle; this is the same for a horse and should be kept in mind when both lungeing and riding.

Now try to walk the circle out of balance, leaning inwards and allowing your weight to drop heavily onto your inside leg. Can you feel the lack of flexibility this generates in your leg and pelvis? It becomes difficult to elevate the inside leg when your weight is thrown too heavily onto it. You have to feel balanced and upright to allow the inside leg to come through.

A horse will also have to work energetically with the inside hind leg to propel his body forwards on the circle. Any excess weight taken by the inside hind will require extra effort to push the body mass forward on the path of the circle, effort the horse needs to make to prevent his inside shoulder leaning in on the circle. The horse has to be taught how to move in balance when on the lunge because this will prepare him for carrying the additional weight of the rider.

The Lazy Horse

Some horses are naturally less active than others and we often see riders having to use their legs continually to maintain any impulsion at all on such horses. A horse on the lunge should work with enthusiasm and not be half asleep (Figures 4.6a and b). A lazy horse may be content to lean on the bit and move with a lack of impulsion; if this happens, ensure the side reins are long enough and not making him shorten in his neck. Right from the start of a horse's training, a forward-thinking and active attitude should be encouraged and he should be taught that all work will demand energy; communication of the aids will then be easier when ridden work begins.

4.6a and b – a) Maestu showing a lack of impulsion; b) Maestu showing a forward-thinking and active attitude

Some horses have a good carriage with steady gaits and will get into a rhythm that makes them look as if they are working well but it may be that they are not using their true vitality and we can assess this by using the following methods.

1   A horse working in trot correctly should move with his hind limbs stepping up into the tracks of the forefeet. If his hind feet do not come sufficiently forwards, he will not be working with adequate energy or engagement.

2   While the horse is in trot, ask for a canter transition. If the transition into canter is energetic, the horse is probably working with sufficient power. If he moves into an unbalanced canter, however, and within a few strides drops back into trot, he has not developed enough vigour in his strides. The trot to canter and canter to trot transitions are useful as the canter work will improve the quality of the trot but, in the early stages, do not lunge for more than a few canter strides because on a circle this gait presents balance difficulties for an uneducated horse.

3   Through lungeing we can establish the energy we seek to motivate the horse to work correctly. It is far easier to do this with a lunge whip reinforcing our commands, than to have a direct confrontation when

in the saddle. He will soon learn that work means work but he will reap the rewards of praise and pride in pleasing his trainer.

4   Initially, a fast pace can be asked of a lazy horse just to wake him up and bring about some energetic movement.   Then when he is mentally tuned to the work, he can be allowed to steady his stride, just as long as he maintains his energy.

Trotting Poles

Trotting poles are of great value in lunge work. We can begin the lunge session as usual without side reins, and then spend several minutes working with the side reins fitted. When the horse is warmed up, he can progress to working over the poles, for which the side reins should either be removed or lengthened so that the horse is not restricted as he lowers his neck to look at the poles. The horse's suppleness will improve if he is worked equally on both reins with frequent changes of direction.

Stepping over poles induces more activity and flexion of a horse's limbs. The increased mobility and flexion of the joints will enable the spine to function with more fluidity, thus improving his athleticism.

Pole work is useful for horses who forge ahead and have a tendency to overtrack with the hind limbs. The poles can be placed either in a straight line or on a circle to assist these horses to elevate and shorten the stride rather than lengthen. Observe how the horse has to adjust his stride to negotiate the poles and space them accordingly. Place about four or five poles on a circle of about 15 m, spacing them about 1 m (3 ft) apart for trot work (the spacing is the same for work on a straight line). Keep the lunge line a little slack whilst the horse is negotiating the poles – but not so slack that he could trip over it – so that his head is not restricted. He has to concentrate on his stride between the poles, trying to maintain balance, and should have no interference from the trainer and the lunge line.

Once the pole work has been successfully completed, a horse can be schooled over a grid of small jumps on the lunge (Figure 4.7).

4.7 Maestu jumping on the lunge

Lungeing can be a useful part of training and can further enhance our harmonious relationship with the horse. Because you are schooling the horse from the ground, many problems can be observed more easily and then worked through calmly. The horse is also being well prepared for the next stage of training: the work in-hand.

The Royal School in Jerez: work between the pillars (photo: Rafael Laemos)

Chapter Five

Working the Horse
In-hand

'Guide, challenge and direct the horse, but always as his trusted friend.'
Jenny Rolfe

During the time spent on loose work and lungeing, a horse will have built up a relationship of confidence and trust with his handler and this will prove a good basis for the next stage: work in-hand. In-hand work has been practised for centuries in the classical school and is an important keystone for the advancement of obedience and suppleness. A trainer can work closely with, and teach so much to, a horse from the ground and this will help to avoid some of the conflicts and misunderstandings that might arise during the ridden work. Piaffe, for example, is one of the high-school movements that can be taught more easily in-hand.

Historically, placing the horse between the pillars, one of the original methods of classical training, has been the most effective way to teach collection and the high-school movements and is still used today by very experienced trainers (Figure 5.1). The horse is tied between two pillars

5.1 A stallion of the Portuguese School performs levade

and encouraged to use his energy to develop athletic and elevated strides. Collection and cadence can be achieved by cultivating the upward 'spring' in the movement. The horse will gradually lower his hindquarters and 'sit' into the movement, thus becoming lighter in the shoulders and forehand.

By working the horse in-hand, the trainer uses his body language as a 'moveable pillar', thus forming a 'boundary' that restricts the horse in his forward movement. This directs the horse's energy towards gaining the necessary elevation and cadence.

This work demands a more intimate relationship between horse and handler than the work in the pillars, with the handler using body language, voice and whip for communication.

Already we have talked about the importance of space and respect, both for ourselves and the horse. In-hand work gives us an opportunity to reinforce this code. We will have close contact with the horse from the ground but he will not be allowed to invade our personal space. He must be encouraged to work, always towards us, in close proximity but must

Teach the horse with confidence

be respectful and aware of our leadership and direction at all times. He will be able to gain confidence from the close contact with the handler and can learn to work with energy, with a greater understanding of the whip and voice aids; the touch of the whip will eventually be replaced by the leg aids of the rider.

In-hand work allows a horse to learn lateral movements in his natural carriage without the additional weight of a rider; it helps him to move easily, actively and effectively, and to become light and balanced.

It is of primary importance that the horse is straight, with the hind legs stepping directly into the path of the forelegs, before he is asked for more collection. If the horse's body-weight is not equally distributed over his haunches, it is physically impossible for him to achieve collection and balance. In the development of collection, the haunches are required to take more of the horse's body-weight and thus have to absorb more of the movement and balance. It could, therefore, damage the horse if his spine is not aligned and there is an imbalance of weight to one side.

Great patience is required to teach the horse slowly to accept the new commands and understand what is required of him. At first, just short sessions will be sufficient, and the aim is to finish on a good note when the horse has responded well and understood his lesson.

The key to successful riding is to encourage the horse to be calm and also to move energetically. This principle applies equally to in-hand training. We are looking for elevation and spring in the strides, and so the horse must learn to move in lightness and self-carriage. The horse should move forwards actively on the instruction of the handler. It is equally important for him to come back to halt when the whip is placed quietly against his neck or croup.

When I was training with *Mestre* Luis Valenca, he commented that Maestu, my stallion, had a magnificent neck and shoulders, well-muscled and impressive, but nature had not given him quite the same muscle on his quarters. He therefore recommended work in-hand to help Maestu to become more strong, supple and athletic when using his hind limbs.

No horse has a perfect conformation and temperament and so training is a way to make the most of what nature has given him and to enhance his natural athletic ability. In-hand work provides excellent suppling exercises to help him do that.

In-hand Equipment

The horse should be tacked up as for a lungeing session with the following equipment.

- Snaffle bridle (a double bridle may be appropriate with an experienced trainer).
- Cavesson and lead rope.

- Roller/saddle.
- Side reins.
- Exercise boots.
- Whip.
- Lunge line (for later exercises).

The side reins should be fitted, equal in length, allowing the horse his natural head and neck carriage. As with lungeing, we do not want to make the horse feel restricted but to allow the top line of the neck to arch with the lower neck muscles relaxed. The head should be carried proudly just in front of the vertical.

Goals for In-hand Work

- To teach the young horse submission and to develop further understanding of the voice and body language (Figure 5.2).
- To familiarize the horse with the whip so that he shows respect but not fear.
- To increase mobility of the shoulder and hind legs (quarters)
- To prepare the horse physically and mentally to receive a rider.
- To give a good grounding beneficial for all future work.
- To develop collection and, later in training, to prepare the horse for high-school movements.

Use of the Whip

The whip is used to reinforce communication with the horse and certainly not as a form of punishment. It may tell him to 'work forwards', 'give more energy' or 'whoa' but it should never be used in frustration or anger. If a particular exercise does not succeed then we need to halt and re-evaluate our methods. The whip is just an extension of a positive, re-enforcing connection with the horse. When humans resort to bullying and violence, this is another way of saying that reasonable and harmonious communication no longer exists. We want the horse to obey our commands but we need to use our knowledge and thought processes to achieve these goals. Once the horse is responding through fear and anxiety, the art of horsemanship has been abandoned. Anyone can become a bully, but bullying is not the way for a student of classical horsemanship, whether the work is being conducted from the ground or the saddle. Our self-control and positive teaching will become the motivation for the horse to cooperate willingly with us.

The whip may be used to communicate in three different ways when working the horse in-hand.

1 To encourage forward movement. A light touch or tap will say, 'take a step forward'.

2 To ask for halt. When one handler is working from the front of the horse, the whip lightly rested on the neck indicates 'whoa' or 'halt' (Figure 5.3). (When the horse has two handlers, if the second handler is using the whip to encourage activity of the hind limbs, with piaffe for example, the whip is

5.2 Working the horse in-hand teaches the horse further understanding of the voice and body language

The whip is an extension of positive re-enforcement

5.3 Place the whip lightly on the neck to indicate halt

placed lightly on the quarters to indicate 'halt'.) This action together with a voice command of a deep, 'ahhr' will be the signal for halt. The whip should remain lying against the horse until he responds and once he has come to a halt, the pressure of the whip should be removed from his body. This command will be taken over by the rider's legs in the ridden work. The rider will place his legs on the girth to ask for halt and as soon as the horse responds, the legs are immediately relaxed.

3   To create energy in movement. In more advanced work the whip may be used with 'electric' tap taps on the hind leg below the hock to produce more activity for such movements as piaffe and passage.

Commencing In-hand Work

Walk and halt

Position yourself with the horse on the long side of the school and prepare to walk on the left rein. Stand calmly with a relaxed body posture in front of, and facing, the horse with the lead rope from the cavesson in the left hand and the whip in the other. The horse is then encouraged to walk towards you and so be prepared to step backwards to allow the horse enough room to move in your direction. With your voice command 'walk on' and small vibrations of the rope, encourage the horse to take a few steps forward. Walk backwards very slowly and, after a few strides, take a deep inward breath and stand tall. Use the voice and whip to halt: a soothing 'ahhr' or 'whoa' (rather than the word 'halt') together with the whip lightly pressed against the neck, will be the command. When the horse recognizes the instruction and halts, praise him with your voice and a gentle stroke on his neck. When working in-hand, it is important that the horse always works towards his handler in order to promote a forward-thinking horse. Repeat the whole exercise by asking the horse to walk forwards for a few more strides, giving your chosen voice command to halt, laying the whip gently on his neck and, as soon as he halts, stroking his neck.

Instruct, perform the exercise and then reward

When the horse has halted is it is important to take the whip away from his body and lower it gently. The quietly given instruction and aids will always be his reward for obedience. He should remain calmly in halt until given further instructions. These new training methods may cause the horse to become tense and so it is important to communicate with your voice, body language and breathing to help him to relax. If he shows tension when standing still, a stroke on the neck together with a deep sigh will calm him. He will sense your relaxed mood and begin to mirror your feelings if you have built up a bond of trust with him.

These basic techniques should be practised for only a few minutes on the left rein and then be repeated on the right rein. The horse may not respond in the same way when you change the direction. Horses, like humans, are one sided and coordination can take longer depending on which rein he is on.

Every effort made by a horse must be rewarded with praise, and the pace of the work must be slow and calm at all times. When he is doing this basic exercise well on a straight line, work can begin on a circle.

Introducing lateral work on the circle

The introduction of these exercises on the circle will help to improve control of the horse's shoulders and activity of his hindquarters.

If you are preparing to circle left, you must position yourself in front of and to the side of the horse and turn to face him (Figure 5.4).

You will need to be in a position to look into his inside eye and, with your eye contact and body position, be prepared to block his forward path. Your body becomes a substitute for the pillars. Initially, it is a good idea to have a helper until the horse becomes familiar with the exercises. The extra handler will assist the mobilization of the hind legs on the circle.

The horse's head should not be allowed to tilt but remain in the vertical position. Luis Valenca Rodrigues used gentle neck flexions before the in-hand work, but this has to be done by an experienced trainer or with an experienced trainer present. Neck flexions relax and stretch the neck muscles; a tilting head may be caused by a 'tight' restricted neck.

The handler aligns himself with, and faces, the horse's neck and shoulders. To circle to the left, for example, the horse should be held with

5.4 Work in-hand: encourage the horse to inscribe a large circle with the hind limbs moving around the forehand

the left hand with his head and neck flexed to the inside. Holding the whip in the right hand, use your voice, body language and whip to ask the horse to commence walking a circle around you. His inside limbs should cross laterally in front of the outside limbs and the front legs should cross over as if performing a turn on the forehand. The hind limbs take larger strides to move the quarters around the forehand, which moves on a smaller circle. The assistant can stand facing the inside hind limb and by tapping it below the hock with the whip can instigate movement, both forward and across. When the inside hind limb is correctly positioned it creates elevation through the back (Figure 5.5). The joints in the hind limbs increase their flexion to increase the capacity of the hind limbs to support more weight, thus allowing a lightening of the shoulders.

After a few strides, ask for halt by laying the whip quietly on the neck and giving a soft voice command, and then repeat the exercise, again just asking for a few strides.

Be prepared to move a step or two backwards as the horse circles

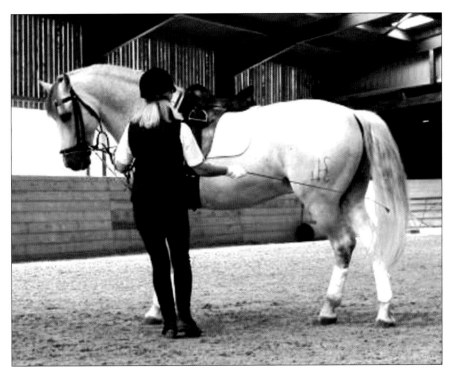

5.5 The correct positioning of the inside hind limb creates elevation through the back

around you. He must have sufficient space to allow movement forwards then across from his inside shoulder. If he is given too little room for movement, he may take a backward step which is totally incorrect; he must be encouraged to be forward-thinking.

Work in-hand directs the energy of the horse into elevation to create collection rather than into the forward movement which is his natural inclination.

Encourage the horse to be forward-thinking

When this exercise is carried out correctly the horse will begin to move in better balance, with the hind limbs becoming more athletic. He will demonstrate greater elasticity of movement and his strides will promote more elevation and self-carriage. These movements should be carried out with steady precision to maximize the potential for true cadence.

This small circle exercise should be executed near the long side of the school. So that, when you reach the outside track again the horse can be taken up the long-side in shoulder-in (Figure 5.6).

5.6 A small circle to the track followed by shoulder-in along the track

In-hand work requires intense concentration from both horse and handler and these exercises should be carried out for just a few minutes at a time. It is possible to correct many problems by using these skills (shoulder stiffness, inactivity of hind limbs, lack of concentration, a lack of understanding of the use of aids and whip, for example), whether the horse is in the early stages of training or at the more advanced levels of work.

Once the horse is familiar with the work on small circles other exercises can be used to further mobility of his shoulders and to develop more engagement.

All these exercises can later be performed with a rider on his back; the rider's leg replaces the handler's whip and the horse will already have a good understanding of the work from his training from the ground. Thus the horse is well prepared for the natural progression from in-hand to ridden work.

Developing Piaffe

This more advanced work in hand can be undertaken when the horse can naturally bring both calmness and energy to this work. To introduce these exercises too soon will only promote unwanted stress in the training. Physically the horse needs to be sufficiently developed to cope with the increased collection demanded for piaffe.

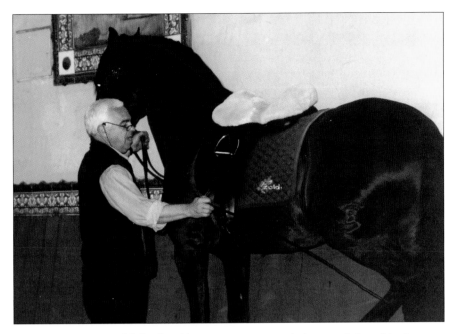

5.7 Maestu learns to lift his hind leg in response to a light tap of the whip. Later this technique will encourage correct placing of the hind limbs for further engagement

The initial lesson should only direct the horse to position his hind limbs correctly at this stage (Figure 5.7). The horse should stand calmly whilst the handler gives quick, light 'electric' taps to the hind leg, below the hock, to ask him to lift one leg at a time in response to the whip. Once the horse has assimilated this lesson, the next stage is to ask him to lift a hind leg and place it well underneath his body because this is the positioning required for future movements in collection. Every time he does this, he must be rewarded.

It is helpful to work with two handlers; one to motivate and control the horse from the front, with a short rope from the cavesson, and the second to stand facing the hind limbs controlling their movements using a schooling whip.

To prepare for this exercise place the horse on the long side of the school and ensure that he is working on a straight line. The aim is to get the horse to shorten his walk by taking half strides forward and so the first handler contains the energy by allowing the horse to take only short strides forward but, when you begin the exercise, it is important that the horse does walk forward and not on the spot. The second handler will again use light, electric touches with the whip on the horse's hind legs to persuade him to place his hind legs, one at a time, further underneath his body. This will influence the horse to elevate through the spine, placing him correctly to cope with the extra weight being distributed over the hind limbs, important requirements for executing piaffe.

After several sessions consolidating this work, begin to ask for a little more. The assistant handler encourages more energy with the light taps to the hind limbs and guides the horse's energy into elevation and upward movement with the maximum flexion of the hind joints.

If the horse becomes unsettled, the exercise should be stopped to allow the horse to calm down again. The aim is to develop steady diagonal movement whilst nurturing a confident energetic attitude, not an anxious stressed mind. Excess tension will cause the back to tighten and restriction of movement will result in stilted strides lacking in co-ordination and rhythm.

Gradually the horse will begin to develop a rhythm in his stride and relax, absorbing more of the weight with his hindquarters. The second handler, positioned towards the back of the horse, will be using the whip to either instigate movement or ask for halt; once the horse has begun to give just a few strides of piaffe, he will prepare to halt the exercise by using the soothing voice tone, 'ahhr', and placing the whip against the horse's croup. As soon as he has come to a halt, the pressure of the whip is removed and he should be rewarded well.

Progress can be made more successfully by asking the horse for just a little at a time, then making much of him when he responds. He may then begin to settle into the work with confidence. When a horse is being taught new movements, things rarely go according to a plan. Both horse and handler will make mistakes with interpretation and communication. Part of the learning process requires that we have to endure many mistakes and the art of learning is the way in which we respond to the lessons learnt. We may not achieve all our goals in a specific time frame, but there is always another day. Two minds are working together, each with their individual concepts of understanding; but this is the joy of the work, learning the art of communication.

These exercises will help to bring about a great improvement in the self-carriage and lightness of the horse, if correctly executed. When the ridden work is commenced the horse will be well prepared for the rider, both mentally and physically. The development of this sense of 'feel' will, over a period of time, become like dancing with a horse who moves with you in true balance and harmony.

Well-executed in-hand work can lead to impressive results in ridden work for both horse and rider. A feeling of oneness and empathy may be gained, which may not have been successfully achieved if this stage had been neglected. The relationship between horse and rider will have been enhanced and the ridden work should simply be a further extension of the training that is already well understood and accepted by the horse.

Balance and harmony (photo: Rafael Lemos)

Chapter Six

Master the Balance and Master the Horse

'Let us walk softly on the Earth, with all living beings, great and small —
remembering as we go, that one God, kind and wise created all'.
Native American blessing

Whilst I was in Lisbon, Antonio Borba Monteiro frequently used the words, 'master the balance and you master the horse'. All gaits and movements require that both horse and rider learn to move together with a natural flow and balance. A rider immediately disturbs a horse's natural balance. The art of balanced riding is to become aware of your own poise and equilibrium and this will allow you to feel 'at one' with the movement and spirit of the horse; horse and rider in perfect harmony.

How is this flow and balance accomplished? Look at the physical requirements of balance, and the harmony needed between our body, mind and spirit. True balance will require harmony between both the physical and the spiritual: the physical body will achieve a balanced state only when the mind and spirit allow a 'centred' and harmonious feeling.

It is not easy to walk into the stable feeling truly relaxed and in the

Create a harmonious balance of body, mind and spirit

right frame of mind to harmonize instantly with a horse every day. It is all too easy to just let things happen around us and not be aware of their effect on our equilibrium. If you can learn to understand your own nature, you can be more effective in your communication with your horse.

The rider's body may appear to an onlooker to be aesthetically balanced but if the mind is full of technical information or negative thoughts the true artistic harmony and oneness will not be revealed. When you study a dance partnership, it may give the impression of being artistic and visual, but it is the unseen bond and the spiritual empathy which is capable of creating the magic.

Human nature can sometimes create its own problems as many people are sceptical about believing what they cannot see. Imagine you are looking across the vast oceans to view the horizon. The line of the horizon is only the boundary of our vision, an imaginary line, which limits our understanding of what may lie beyond. We can always limit our horizon to what has been proven. Scientific minds might find it hard to believe in a dimension of life that defies a technical explanation.

Similarly, it is too easy to limit our understanding of the awareness and intelligence of the horse. After many years of communicating with the horse, however, I have discovered that human preconceptions can hold us back. Several years ago if someone had told me that they could gain a response from a horse by just becoming aware of their breathing, I have to admit that I would have been sceptical and, without thinking, was thus placing limitations on the mind and sensitivity of the horse. When the rider is receptive to the true nature of the horse, communication can become almost telepathic and if this nature is unravelled,

Don't limit your personal horizons

harmony and balance can evolve. The horse has an intelligent, sensitive and spiritual nature and we need to think in terms of mind-to-mind communication, which a horse will understand.

A professional sportsman may develop his own style within his sport and this may be equally as successful as another; every personality will look for a slightly different approach. The equestrian sport and art involves not only a human but also a horse, another living creature who brings individuality of thought and emotional response to the partnership.

We should be prepared to learn something new each day about ourselves and our horses. This is an exciting adventure which can have a fundamental effect on the whole of our lives. We have an opportunity to use our individuality, instincts and spirit to enhance the training and understanding of our horses.

We all need education and stimulation to progress, but too much teaching can produce a rider who is not communicating on a one-to-one basis with a horse but through an interpreter, the trainer, who can only view the picture, as he sees it, from the ground and may not be aware of what the rider is feeling. The rider may be giving direction to the horse as a result of listening to the trainer and not the horse. There needs to be time for both and once the rider feels more confident in his ability, it could be beneficial to spend some time alone with a horse to consolidate the lessons. On the contrary, the aspiring horseman can of course gain much wisdom and inspiration from gifted trainers, authors and riders.

I have a great love for paintings and the variety of style, technique, colour and composition is infinite. If twenty artists were asked to study and paint the same subject, you would see twenty individual interpretations of the same theme. We can feel inspired by watching talented riders and trainers and if we look carefully at each one, we will see many variations of technique. All of us are physically different as well as being mentally unique and if we all follow the same pattern of training our interpretation might not reflect our individuality. Neither we nor a horse will perform to the best of our abilities if we perform as puppets.

The horse performing the more advanced dressage movements in his natural environment is expressing his excitement or pride (Figure 6.1). In training, we expect a horse to reproduce these movements mechanically but ignore the feelings and emotions that would stimulate them naturally. This is why it is important for the horse to enjoy his work because only then can his freedom of spirit give true *joie de vivre* and creativity to a performance.

Good trainers can give inspiration and impart knowledge to pupils and can help with discipline, accuracy, focus, the value of the rider's position and the relevance of different school exercises. Equally, time

6.1 Ebanisto – a natural expression of exuberance and pride

Recapture
forgotten
skills

spent alone with a horse can teach other important lessons. When studying communication with horses, I have experienced the value of listening solely to the horse and the importance of timing. These calmer moments have given me the opportunity to create more feel in riding and to develop more patience!

Important Learning Steps for the Rider

As the journey of horsemanship unfolds, we realize how much there is to learn. Once we understand the importance of being more aware of the horse, we can begin to master the art of balance both physically and mentally. It is extremely important for us to have physical stability and balance, and so it is essential to have a saddle that fits the horse correctly; this will help the rider to achieve a good, balanced position.

The rider's early training should, ideally, take place on the lunge so that he can concentrate on the horse and his movement. Many hours of ridden work on the lunge will help to develop a more 'feeling' balanced seat, capable of flowing with the horse through his different gaits with a natural balance. I call this the 'passive' seat.

A rider needs to develop a passive seat in order to have a positive influence on the horse. Once this becomes established, it will be possible to help the horse to readjust his balance as necessary and make progress with his training. Some problems encountered when riding can stem from the inadequate fitness and suppleness of the rider.

There are no short cuts for the dedicated rider and it can take years to understand the various techniques that give us the ability to influence the balance of the horse. Sometimes it may only be a lightening and easing of the seat that can take enough pressure from the horse's back so that he gains the confidence to relax and lift his spine.

It could be, for example, that a horse always finds a particular corner of the school spooky and approaches it with tension and stilted strides. The rider can learn how to relax his seat, slow the rhythm of his back and redistribute his weight to steady the horse. It may just be a case of learning when the horse needs the security of the rider's leg to encourage him forwards when he instinctively wants to back away. We are always learning to adapt our balance and seat to gain the response we seek.

If we look at our body awareness and posture, we can begin to understand how our poise and breathing can affect the horse. We are all different in our body shapes and hence we hold our tension in different places. The techniques of yoga, Pilates, the Alexander technique or physiotherapy all have their place in helping us to achieve deeper and calmer mental attitudes, suppleness and good posture. It is interesting to observe the body poise and artistry in the martial arts; body movements are centred and flow in an amazingly balanced way. It is possible to achieve a similar energy flow in your riding which will enhance your performance and the comfort of your horse.

Breathing and Realignment

Riders should take every opportunity to think about their posture. Below are some helpful breathing techniques to help you develop more focus, balance and body awareness.

Exercises out of the saddle
LATERAL BREATHING

Standing with your feet about 46 cm (18 in) apart, take a deep breath inwards; feel your ribcage expand and widen and your body grow taller. Let the breath flow to the sides of your ribs and into your spine, not upwards. Relax slowly on the outward breath allowing the ribcage to relax and feel the breath ripple through the upper body and lower abdomen.

Continue with your steady inhaling and exhaling.

Breathe deeply and widely

With each breath inward expand the body slightly, growing taller with each breath. Let the inward breath lengthen and widen your body. Allow the outward breath to relax the ribcage and feel the tension release between your shoulders.

Looking forward, directly in front of you, squeeze the muscles tightly around your eyes then slowly release the pressure and relax. This softens the eyes (i.e. softens the focus) and the facial muscles. Pull your chin backwards gently towards the back of the neck (double chins may appear) then relax. This exercise will help realign the vertebrae in the neck.

Bring both shoulders up towards your head and gently circle them backwards, downwards and then forwards, allowing them to relax back and down naturally. Hold the inward breath for a few seconds. Then gently exhale and feel the air ripple through your spine and abdomen. Coughing helps you to 'feel' the correct muscles, which can be 'scooped' or 'squeezed' upwards, then tighten them to feel the core of stability that can be created.

Continue breathing deeply in the way described until you can really feel the breathing creating a vigorous centre in the lower abdomen. This core of strength will be well able to support the upper torso, not only with stability but also with the ability to create energy flow. This will be the key to carrying out transitions when you are riding, not the strong leg or the driving seat. You will influence your horse with your breathing and harmony.

BODY AWARENESS

For the next exercise let the arms hang down loosely. Allow the shoulders to relax and the chest to expand lifting the ribcage; the ribcage lifts as a result of lateral breathing and not the forward arching of the spine. The sternum (breast bone) should remain relaxed and not tightened or pushed forward. In this way the shoulders fall back more naturally allowing your upper body more space. The upper arm (shoulder to elbow) can hang with its weight dropped down only as far as the elbow; the lower arm (elbow to wrist) should have a lighter feel. Lift the lower arm, from the elbow (as if holding reins in front of you). Clench the fists and tighten the muscles in your arms. Now relax, allow the weight to drop into the elbows and lighten your lower arms from the elbow to the wrist. Feel the lightness in the lower arm, in the wrist and hand. This is the feel to be developed when riding.

The following points will assist body awareness.

- Softening the facial muscles and the focus of the eyes.
- Have the feeling of filling the space around you. Grow taller and expand your posture allowing your head to come forward and upwards. Do not tighten the back of the neck but allow it to lengthen whilst keeping a relaxed jaw. Create a feeling from within of pride and self assurance.
- Cultivate the feeling that your head is balanced in lightness, floating above the shoulders, as a balloon above your body (Figure 6.2).
- Release the tension in your neck, looking left then right very slowly.
- Keep the softer feel in the breast bone whilst breathing and widening the chest (not by pushing the ribcage outwards but by breathing 'into your spine').

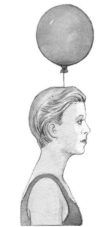

6.2 The head feels weightless like a balloon

- Feel the centre of energy created through the abdominal breathing. Lengthen the spine, and ensure the upper torso is in self-carriage, supported by the waist and abdominal muscles.
- Allow the shoulders to come back and down in a relaxed, comfortable (not forced) manner; this will allow natural expansion and elevation of your upper body through lateral breathing.
- The arms from the shoulder to the elbow form part of the strong centre. Allow weight to drop into a relaxed elbow.
- The arms from the elbow to hand are light in order to hold the reins with feel.
- The feet should be placed slightly apart and allow the knee joints to be released not locked.
- The whole person should feel energized with a feeling of poise and pride.

IMPROVING FLEXIBILITY AND MOVEMENT

The following exercises help you to improve posture, strength and suppleness. They can increase your awareness of areas where you hold tension and where there is stiffness and a lack of mobility. Throughout any exercises, focus on deep rhythmical breathing and feeling comfortable within the exercise. The preparation for these exercises will be the breathing and body awareness routines above.

If we practise these exercises regularly, the benefits will be:
- greater self-awareness and balance – an enhancement of wellbeing
- improvement in suppleness
- more poise in our natural posture
- enhancement of riding ability and position.

Exercise 1 – arm swing

Prepare by standing in a relaxed way and centring your posture and breathing. With your feet about 46 cm (18 in) apart and arms hanging loosely by your side, swing your body slowly to the left and then swing back round to the right (Figures 6.3a and b). Allow your arms to swing loosely away from your body. Continue this exercise several times until you feel loose and relaxed in the upper body.

6.3a and b Exercise 1: arm swing

Exercise 2 – *arm stretch*

Continue with your deep breathing and raise your arms high above your head, clasping your hands together. Stretch upwards and allow your upper body to gently arch slightly backwards (Figure 6.4). With your knees slightly bent and relaxed, stand on your toes and stretch your whole body up, up, up, towards your clasped hands. Take a deep breath inwards and on the outward breath, relax and slowly release your hands. Lower your arms to your sides. Repeat this exercise several times.

6.4 Exercise 2: arm stretch above head

Exercise 3 – *touching your toes*

Stand with feet about 46 cm (18 in) apart and commence deep abdominal breathing. Raise your arms above your head, then take your arms out in front of you and allow your upper body to follow the movement. Slowly allow your arms to drop towards the ground bringing your upper body and head slowly forwards and downwards until you are able to touch your toes (Figures 6.5a and b). If this is uncomfortable, only work and stretch within your comfort zone. Stay in this position for a few

6.5a and b Exercise 3: touching your toes

Relax into
the exercises

moments, breathing deeply, and then uncurl your spine, very slowly, as you straighten your body, raising your neck and head last to complete this exercise.

Exercise 4 – leg stretch

Repeat the previous exercise and when you are relaxed and touching your toes, place both hands on the floor in front and to either side of your feet, bending the knees if necessary. Take a deep breath in and on the outward breath, put one leg out behind you (Figure 6.6). Really stretch the leg out pressing your weight against the ball of your foot. Feel the stretch in your inner thigh and calf muscles. After a few moments, take a deeper breath

6.6 Exercise 4: leg stretch

inwards and bring your leg back next to the other one so that your feet are together and your hands remain on the floor.

Now take the other leg back and feel the stretch for a few moments before returning to your hands-on-the-floor position with both feet together. This exercise may be repeated several times and then, slowly, whilst breathing outwards, uncoil your spine to return to an upright position and stand with good posture.

This exercise is most beneficial for the rider as it stretches and tones the inner thigh and leg muscles which will help to stabilize the riding position in a relaxed and natural way. This will enable you to develop a more independent pelvis and seat, whilst your legs hang naturally and loosely down against the sides of the horse.

These are just a few beneficial stretches, but there are several yoga and Pilates routines that can aid strength and suppleness for the rider. A study of tai chi, or Feldenkrais movements and dancing can help to develop more flexibility, which for riders is particularly helpful for core stability and strength.

The ancient Chinese and Indian civilizations believed that the centre of energy, in the body, is just below the navel area. If our breathing can help to enhance this awareness, then the rider can gain a more centred and balanced feeling. Once the rider is sitting on the back of the horse, an awareness of this important centre will help the horse and rider to master the balance.

Exercises in the saddle

Once you are in the saddle, take a few moments to practise the previous breathing patterns and think quietly about poise and posture. Use only a quiet horse who is safe and reliable for the exercises below. Have an experienced handler with you to hold the horse when you are working at a standstill, or to lunge you when you exercise on the move, so that you can focus solely on yourself and have no concerns about the horse.

Quieten and focus the mind

Here is a very useful exercise to practise whilst the horse is standing still. Sit in the normal position in the saddle with both of your hands placed on the pommel. Bring both knees up in front of you in the style of a jockey (Figure 6.7). Feel the stretch, for maybe twenty seconds and then slowly lower the legs, one at a time, taking them out and away from the saddle. Allow the legs to lower gently and, when fully lowered, to nestle against the saddle. You will feel the stretch of the inner thigh muscles, which will help your legs to feel longer and more relaxed, thus giving you more stability in the saddle.

With focused, lateral breathing your body will be in a good posture.

6.7 Legs up jockey style

Allow your seat to relax into the saddle, with a feel of 'melting' and 'allowing'. This is not slumping or slouching but a freedom of movement within a good posture mobility within core stability.

EXERCISE TO DEVELOP NATURAL BALANCE

The handler should stand with, or hold, the horse whilst the rider continues with these breathing exercises.

1   Take a deep breath inwards and, on the outward breath, gradually lean your body forwards as far as you feel comfortable (Figure 6.8a).

2   Take another breath inwards and steadily bring your body back to the upright position.

3   Slowly, on the outward breath, lean backwards as far as you feel comfortable, arching and lengthening your back (Figure 6.8b).

Continue breathing as described and moving the upper body slowly backwards and forwards. Each time the exercise is repeated, make less backward and forward movement; the body should look like a pendulum that is slowly swinging less and less.

Gradually the movement will become almost insignificant and you will feel a moment when you 'arrive' in a natural balance. This is what you need to feel to help you understand your natural balance whilst the horse

6.8a Pendulum exercise: leaning forward

6.8b, Pendulum exercise: leaning backwards

is standing still. Every movement of the horse will affect your balance, and riding on the lunge will aid your progress towards mastering your balance.

RIDING ON THE LUNGE – FEELING THE MOVEMENT

- The horse has forward locomotion and also sideways movement. If you stand behind a horse whilst he is moving away from you, you can observe the sideways swing: watch the ribcage and the hindquarters move gently from side to side.

- When moving on a circle, the outside limbs of the horse will track a slightly larger circle than the inside limbs. This means that the horse will have to stretch the muscles on the outside of his body and slightly contract and relax those on the inside.

- This will help to engage the inside hind leg, as the horse will have to use more strength from this leg to propel himself around the circle.

- The walk should be a regular four-beat gait, the trot is a two-beat gait and the canter is a three-beat gait.

- Try to pick up on the rhythm within the gait, allowing your strong centre and pelvis to gently absorb both the sideways and forward

Feel the sideways and forward movement

movement. Imagine sitting on a space hopper or on a swing; neither will move unless you activate them. Think about sitting on the hopper and the movement needed to create a bounce. This can help the rider to be more aware of the absorption needed within movement. The horse is not a static object and so the rider must think about tuning in to a 'bounce' or movement and creating a more absorbing seat.

Our body position is not just about relaxation, it is about support and positive energy.

Whilst riding on the circle, the rider's upper body will be directing the horse on to the correct track of the circle and the rider's seat is balanced to absorb and mirror the movement; remember that the inside limbs of the horse will be tracking slightly shorter strides. Your legs should hang down loosely (like wet flannels) so that if a plumb line was dropped from the top of your head, it would pass down through your body to your feet. The position is that of standing with slightly flexed knees; if the horse were taken away from under you, you would land on your feet. This position of balance is similar to that used when skiing.

The position of the rider's shoulders can have a significant effect on the balance of the horse. The shoulders should be relaxed, yet poised. The release of tension in the shoulders will allow the ribcage and chest to expand and 'balloon', which will help the upper body to maintain good self-carriage and provide a greater ability to absorb the motion of the horse. The feeling is one of riding from 'stomach (or waist) to hand', with the seat advancing. When you walk up the stairs you elevate through the leg and knee to take the first step to moving forward and upward. The second step is created from a lift of the whole body. When riding, this forward and upward motion begins from the seat; the seat and lower back allow for increased absorption and mobility, thus compensating for the movement.

To position the horse to work correctly on the circle, you may need at times to ask for more inside flexion. Turn your shoulders slightly, bringing your inside shoulder back a little further. When you reposition your inside shoulder slightly further back, you will feel the release of the inner thigh. If at this point you use your inside leg to 'tap, tap' just behind the girth, it will encourage the horse to further engage and develop a lighter self-carriage.

The outside hand and leg will contain the outside of the horse and ensure he does not swing his quarters out away from the direction of the circle. Ride a couple of strides in this way then ride the horse forwards. If these aids were continued with emphasis on the inside hind, the work would become a lateral exercise. Once the horse is correctly positioned on the circle, with the inside hind engaged, he is asked to move forwards on the circle. Later on, as training progresses, the position of your shoulders and focused breathing will become the major communication tool to ask the horse for shoulder-in.

MEDITATION ON THE LUNGE

The nature of the horse reveals a tendency to rely on his natural, primitive instincts to instigate both thoughts and responses. Humans on the other hand have, over a period of time, evolved very rapidly with the advance of technology and this has resulted in a loss of connection with our 'gut instinct' with less capacity and time for spiritual meditation. If we wish to communicate well with our horses, we have to relearn these skills, which will in turn help us to focus our minds. The quietening of the mind can help us to find harmony both within ourselves and with our horses.

Whilst on the lunge, new thought patterns can be acquired because the handler is controlling the horse; the rider can close his eyes softly and begin to **feel more** and **see less**. Deeper and equally important skills will begin to take over, enhancing the feeling of motion and oneness with the horse. For many of the Native American peoples, for example, their horses were simply an extension of themselves and the natures of man and horse were linked in every aspect of their lives. For most horse owners in the modern world it is too much to expect to be able to connect with the world of horses in the same way when, often, only a short period of each day is spent with their horses.

These techniques, if practised regularly, will help to create a deeper sense of feel and assist us in concentrating our busy minds on listening to and harmonizing with the horse.

TROT WORK ON THE LUNGE

If you use your stirrups to practise the rising trot, here are some points to remember.

- Keep the rise natural, not forced (Figure 6.9).
- Rise forwards, i.e. feel like you are taking your stomach towards your hand, and land lightly in the saddle (like a feather).
- To check you are in balance with your horse stay up for two beats of the trot.
- If, when you land lightly back in the saddle, you find the horse has left you behind, then you are not yet in true balance.
- Become aware of sitting centrally within the movement. Sometimes on a circle your weight can shift too much to the outside. Keep the inner thigh relaxed with sufficient weight in the inside leg to help to maintain a balanced feel.
- Music may be helpful whilst on the lunge; it will enhance your rhythm, concentration and enjoyment. If no music is available try humming or singing!

For the sitting trot do not use your stirrups. You can hold the pommel of the saddle with one hand to help to elevate and stabilize your upper body. Allow your legs to relax and lengthen whilst your seat absorbs the movement from below the waist. The waist should be supported by the abdominal muscles and the spine and not be allowed to collapse.

If the lunge session is progressing calmly, try closing your eyes and concentrating on the feel. A person who is blind will develop a greater awareness of the sounds, feels and smells he encounters. We are sometimes unaware of so much around us because we just focus on what we see, and our other important sensory skills lie dormant. It is sometimes more easy to 'do' than to take time to 'feel'. The harmony between man and horse is rooted in the capacity to tune in and feel.

6.9 In trot work, keep the rise natural, not forced

After much practice on the

lunge you will find that riding passively in self-carriage becomes second nature. Over a period of time you will be able to maintain balance through transitions and gaits with a good ability to absorb, and flow with, the movement. This is the time when you are ready to have a more positive influence on the balance of the horse.

Our body awareness and control is so often neglected and can be linked with problems in training, which are manifested both physically and mentally.

When you initially learn to drive a car you are presented with a wealth of problems that require concentration and coordination. The gear changing, clutch control, steering etc. can take many weeks or months of practice until it all becomes second nature.

We learn our habits, good and bad, through repetition. Over a period of time, good poise and balance, together with a harmonious mind prepared to listen to a horse, will be the result of dedication and practice.

The Young Horse: Working in Balance

There is an old Portuguese proverb which says, 'One hour of play is worth a year of conversation'. This philosophy tells us that if learning is fun and enjoyable for humans and animals, the time spent teaching can become a time to build a relationship.

When the young horse comes out of the stable we must first work him loose or on the lunge before ridden work is commenced. Our first goal is to ensure the horse is gaining confidence and is allowed to work in his natural outline with 'looseness' (freedom) and not tension or restriction. This will be impossible if we confine the natural, forward movement with our hands.

When a horse moves from halt to walk, or walk to trot, his head and neck will need the freedom to move forward. This enables him to carry forward the propulsion of energy from his hind limbs. If his natural head carriage is restricted then his gaits will become stilted. We will be guilty of asking the horse to move forwards with our seat and legs but depriving him of the freedom to propel

One hour of play is worth a year of conversation

No athlete,
whether
human
or horse,
can
perform
with a
tight
restricted
neck and
head

6.10 The rider must encourage the horse to move in a
natural self-carriage

himself forward in a natural way. If the horse is not able to move with a
sense of freedom, he will never be in self-carriage and will become reliant
upon a heavy contact with his mouth (Figure 6.10). No athlete, whether
horse or human, can perform in true, natural balance if he is restricted in
his head and neck; it is a physical impossibility.

If we aim for energetic strides then a harsh contact with the mouth
can only restrict a horse and create tightness. We are trying to encourage
him to move forward freely with confidence in a good, natural rhythm.
The work on the lunge and the in-hand work will help the horse to
understand the correct position for his head and neck. I will cover the
training of the horse in his natural balance in the following chapters.

Master the Balance

Classical horsemanship is all about trying to establish a bond between a
rider and a horse, based on true harmony and balance. We can learn to
master our own self-carriage and thoughts, but we also have the ultimate
responsibility for the wellbeing of the horse. It falls upon our shoulders

to make certain that the horse grows more supple and strong physically, together with developing his confidence and ensuring his peace of mind.

In order to ride in balance and true harmony, much love, respect and devotion must be given to a horse so that he can become a friend who will willingly give his utmost attention and energy in all spheres of riding. A pattern of communication can be built that will give both pleasure and enjoyment. Praise and encouragement will enable the horse to feel proud and gain in confidence. To have a truly balanced horse and rider requires the physical oneness in balance together with a harmonious mental and spiritual connection (Figure 6.11).

It is important to look at our own strengths and weaknesses and how we can build on the positive aspects of our natural ability. Once we have begun the journey of discovery about ourselves, we will be more effective in communicating with our horses. We need to look honestly at our personality, yet be content with who we are. The horse can then respect our individuality and our friendship and, after a period of time, horse and rider can be equally content, sharing a bond of trust and honesty; we will have a horse who enjoys his work and understands fair discipline. These are the fundamental truths that can help us to truly master ourselves and become the master of a horse.

> A happy horse is a balanced horse in body, mind and spirit

6.11 Jenny working with Delfin. Over the years a relationship of trust and understanding has been built up in which Delfin can feel both proud and confident

Self-awareness of our breathing and balance encourages harmony and oneness with a horse (photo: Barrie Rolfe)

Chapter Seven

Breathe Life into Training

'All beings share the power of breathing; learn to understand this essence of life'
Jenny Rolfe

An invaluable contribution has been made to this chapter by Celia Cohen, a chartered human and veterinary physiotherapist, who explains the physiology behind the breathing techniques and also why they can be so effective.

Learning the Power of Breathing within Riding

Mestre Luis Valenca Rodrigues told me that every day he spent with his horses he learnt something new. This is certainly true as, in my experience, every new relationship demands more thought and re-evaluation of my approach. I have learnt the importance of working from the ground using the voice, breathing techniques and body language as a

7.1 The horse can learn about breathing and body language when being trained from the ground; the inward breath is a half-halt rebalancing both horse and trainer

means of communication. When the training is continued under saddle, I have found that more focus and awareness of breathing techniques enhances the natural balance of the rider and the empathy with the horse. The power of learning to breathe within riding can bring a much deeper sense of empathy with the horse which in turn can alleviate tension and stress. (Figure 7.1.)

An awareness of breathing techniques can give us mastery of our mood, balance and co-ordination. A deeper understanding of breathing awareness is already used by professional singers, actors, dancers, athletes and practitioners of martial arts, yoga and a variety of relaxation therapies.

If riders can learn to utilize these skills in horsemanship, then not only does the rider enhance his own performance but also that of the horse. This is already a well-recognized factor in gaining personal control and balance but has been rather neglected and overlooked as a skill that will help the rider. My greatest teacher in building an awareness of the significance of our breathing has been the horse.

This chapter looks at the importance of breathing and how it elicits such an effective response from a horse. Once a horse comprehends both the trainer's breathing and body language from the loose work, it will be highly influential in the way a horse relates to his trainer. I believe this arises from the way in which horses instinctively relate to each other in the herd. Breathing is fundamental to life.

Breathing is a 'language' common to humans and animals and if we can find the techniques to communicate, we can have a profound influence on the frame of mind of other living creatures.

When a baby is born, everyone waits for the newborn to gasp for its first breath, the beginning of a new independent life. From that moment babies and young children will learn to respond to the breathing patterns of their mothers. When my children were very young, if they were distressed I would nurse them in my arms and breathe more deeply to encourage them to sleep.

More recently we acquired a whippet puppy, Lara, who, sadly, is deaf. When she arrived she obviously missed the security of her mother and the rest of the litter. I held her quietly on my lap as she wriggled and whined, hoping that she would relax and become calmer. I decided to treat her as I would an anxious horse and began to breathe more deeply and yawn. Within a few seconds Lara yawned, relaxed and very soon her breathing pattern had altered and she fell asleep.

When we feel fear or are tense, the initial reaction is a change in our pattern and rhythm of breathing; it becomes shallow and rapid and causes changes in our posture and capability for free flowing movement. As we have established, horses are creatures of fear and flight, which means they respond immediately to any form of threat with shallow breathing, tightening of muscles and readiness for escape (Figure 7.2). They have evolved to sense and respond immediately to danger, which makes the horse very aware of changes in breathing patterns. Stress and tension are positive when a flight or fight situation occurs: sweating and increased heart and respiratory rates are all physiological preparations to aid survival. In the absence of physical

Breathing is fundamental to life; a common language to all living creatures

7.2 Horse in high tension

exertion, mild symptoms can still be experienced by humans in response to the everyday stresses in our lives. The long-term effects of stress are known to be detrimental to both our physical and psychological health.

When we try to teach something to a horse who exhibits any of these signs, the teaching process will probably be ineffective. A tense horse in walk and trot can be seen to over-tighten the abdominal muscles and become stiff and rigid in his back. This prevents fluidity of movement and the horse will not be capable of demonstrating either his elegance or suppleness.

My Early Experiences with Breathing Techniques

The art of communicating with breathing first became apparent to me on a very windy day whilst riding Delfin on Exmoor in the south west of England. The mares in the adjoining field were galloping about and creating havoc causing Delfin to become totally distracted from his work. His head was in the air and he strutted around like a peacock!

My seat, leg aids and voice commands were useless and my stress levels rose. My frustration increased and this just added to the electric impulses flowing through Delfin's mind and body. The fine tuning and telepathy I sought had totally disappeared. Have you ever tried to tune a radio into a station with no aerial? I halted and he stood and quivered, ready to release his pent-up energy anywhere and in any way.

Almost subconsciously I took a deep breath inwards, I suppose in exasperation as my communications were having no impact on Delfin, and then I remember breathing outwards quite strongly and slowly. The release of the air brought about a flow of relaxation and energy through my body. My seat lost its tension and my legs became lighter around Delfin's ribcage. He responded immediately: I felt a slight lifting and loosening of his back and he began to concentrate and walk forwards more calmly. I leant forward, stroked his neck and took a breath inwards, Delfin came back to halt. I had not planned this and felt it happened as an instinctive response.

I was extremely curious about the effect my breathing had on Delfin and so I began to repeat these exercises over and over again. He would move from halt to walk or walk to trot when I exhaled deeply and then, with my deeper inward breaths, he responded with downward transitions. I was amazed. He was concentrating much more on my breathing and not so much on the mares and other external influences.

Could these techniques work again? The following day I was eager to repeat them with him to see if I could gain a similar response. The lessons were repeated and, to my delight, remembered and understood. Could they help me to communicate with any other horses, or was it something I would only experience with Delfin? He is an extremely sensitive horse and it was possible that other horses would not pick up such subtle changes in my breathing patterns.

Be prepared to learn something new

To put this to the test, I used these techniques with my bay stallion, Maestu, who has a totally different outlook on life from Delfin, being very laid back but quite assertive and dominant in nature. He can be quite grumpy if he is not the first horse to be worked each day!

Despite the differences in his nature, Maestu quickly understood and responded to the same breathing patterns. This was a breakthrough in my study of communication. I understood the significance of the rider's seat, but I had not thought deeply about the importance of breathing. I now realize that our understanding of breathing is fundamental to control and balance of both our body and seat.

In the following months I rode many horses, of every type and breed, in this same manner. Each one responded very quickly which confirmed my belief that this method of communication is of fundamental importance to riding and training.

Within two days of starting work with a lovely grey Spanish Pure-bred stallion, known on the yard as Floyd, he responded to my breathing when working on the lunge and in his loose work. When I rode him, I used the same techniques when asking for transitions and he immediately responded to my breathing. It seemed to come naturally to him because, being a very sensitive and gentle horse, he preferred the less-is-more school of communication. (Figures 7.3a and b.)

Understanding the Importance of Breathing Techniques

An awareness of how we breathe can have a huge impact on every aspect of our lives. It will enable us to control and master tension and stress. Breathing comes naturally and so we do not consciously need to be concerned about breathing in order to do it, but we can consciously influence the *way* we breathe in order to help our bodies to develop better posture and more fluid movement. Many people are insufficiently aware of the importance of the muscles in the abdominal area and breathe using only the muscles of the upper chest. If the correct abdominal breathing is used when inhaling or exhaling, a core of stability can be created. This helps to locate the correct centre of gravity and

7.3a and b a) Floyd looks at mares in the field while Lucy is focused on her breathing to gain his concentration; b) We talk about core stability as Floyd begins to be more attentive

balance. If a hand is placed on the stomach on the inward breath, it should feel like a balloon being blown up; on the outward breath, the balloon effect will be deflated and the stomach drawn in.

Breathing is not only of fundamental importance to the rider but also to the horse. Horses prefer to be working with us in harmony, founded upon regular and relaxed breathing patterns. If they are relaxed, breathing deeply and rhythmically, they can support themselves and carry a rider with less strain. The body of a horse under these conditions can operate with fluidity and mobility and not be disturbed by incorrect breathing patterns and tension. The spine can relax and lengthen to support the movement.

The following words were written by Alois Podhajsky in his excellent book *The Complete Training of Horse and Rider*.

> The technique of breathing plays an important part in the performance of the horse, in the same way that it does with a human being. This technique will be the result of methodical training and will increase the powers of endurance. Excited horses, which do not carry the weight of their riders correctly, will be sooner out of breath and unable to produce as good a performance as well-trained horses. Regular breathing will reveal to the observer a physically and mentally well-balanced horse stepping with regularity. High blowing is a sign of well-being.

Controlled breathing techniques are very often used to centralize and focus people, especially to help relieve tension and improve self-awareness. When people say, 'you look stressed and uptight', you are transmitting these messages without saying anything verbally: restricted breathing patterns, tight shoulders and facial expressions can say it all. If other people can be aware of this pent-up tension, an intuitive horse will certainly tune in to these feelings.

For a rider, the ability to consciously release tension and focus is vitally important. Breathing control and self-awareness can be extremely useful tools of communication if used with sensitivity. When you think about your breathing, not only do you tend to slow and deepen the rate, but you also instinctively begin to centre and be aware of your core.

The abdominal area just below the navel, is where we need to feel controlled, strong and balanced to allow the arms and legs to work efficiently and accurately.

To become effective and sensitive, whether riding or handling the horse, you must first master your balance and find your personal centre. Breathing awareness and control helps you to find this centre, focus more attention and calm the mind. Your thoughts and actions can become clearer and more sensitive as a result. If we refine our aids in riding, we become more fluid, stable and effective. Strong, physical aids will disrupt the balance of the rider.

Rider Posture and Movement

Riding is a very unnatural activity for the human, whose body is designed, albeit poorly, to walk on two feet and move the body over the feet as they contact the ground. When riding this rotation is mainly through the pelvis and hips. With this is mind it is necessary to look at the human body and its movement and see how this is affected by posture when sitting on a horse.

The human spine

The human spine supports weight like a pillar, unlike the four-legged equine's spine which supports weight like a beam. Every time we sit or stand up, our backs must work against gravity to support a top-heavy structure.

Many things can influence your posture, for example:

* pain
* tension/stress
* repetitive tasks
* body image.

The musculoskeletal system and respiratory system are heavily influenced by the position and posture we are in. When an 'ideal' aligned posture is achieved, no individual structure or system is overstressed or strained. The spine should have a normal S shape which allows the forces of gravity to be overcome efficiently without strain or stress (Figures 7.4a

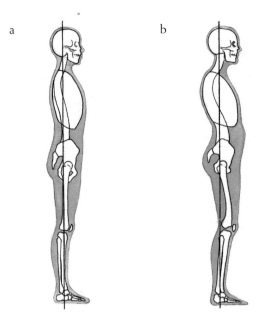

a   b

7.4a and b a) An ideal
balanced posture; b) a
poor unbalanced harmful
posture

ideal plumbline alignment   kyphosis-lordosis

and b). We know that in the human and the horse, if something is uncomfortable and forced, more energy is expended. This is why the stressed or pressured horse sweats excessively for the level of work he is doing and is more likely to suffer injury as a consequence.

Breathing, balance and self-carriage

The body has peripheral receptors and central brain controls that monitor the levels of carbon dioxide in the bloodstream. The fluctuations that occur in this system trigger our breathing. The 'art' of breathing relies upon the mobility within the ribcage and thorax (the part of the trunk between the neck and the abdomen) allowing the inspired air to flow in without resistance. The air is sucked in, in a way comparable to a vacuum cleaner, and the thorax creates a negative pressure which draws the air inwards. The diaphragm (a large sheet of muscle separating the chest from the abdomen) must descend for this to happen. There are accessory muscles which allow a bigger and deeper breath to be taken. For muscles to work well, they need to be in an optimum position (i.e. not over-stretched or over-shortened) free from tension and pain.

Stress and tension as well as stiffness in the thorax, can all impede efficient breathing. Many humans in normal day to day activities have become so unaware of their breathing that they breathe apically, i.e. only using the top third of their lungs, and leave two thirds of the respiratory capacity redundant. If people rarely exert themselves and then suddenly take part in exercise, they soon become breathless. They have lost the ability to control and use the respiratory system efficiently: the power of breathing.

Breathing awareness can enhance both balance and self-carriage, and correct breathing will help supple and strengthen the lower abdominal muscles, which should be utilized to absorb a horse's movement. A rider thus stabilized can help a horse to find his natural balance in movement. He will become very responsive to our core stability.

If a horse becomes too strong in the hand, you should take a sharp, deeper breath inwards, which will enhance your core stability from your lower back. This action will cause the horse to rebalance under you helping him to lighten the forehand and take more weight on the haunches. He will then have the ability to move in a better outline and balance, without leaning on the rider's hands. (Figures 7.5a and b.) By

Breathing enhances balance

concentrating on balance and breathing, together with 'allowing' and 'feeling' hands, we are learning horsemanship in the classical tradition.

Lateral breathing is the key to the half-halt which is the term used for the rebalancing of the horse and rider.

7.5a and b a) Maestu is resisting a connection with the rider's hand, there is insufficient energy in the gait; b) Celia has gained more control of her own core stability. Maestu is working in good balance with sufficient energy and is also more attentive and accepting of a contact

Lateral Breathing

The key to the half-halt

Try this exercise whilst walking.

Walk normally for several strides and then take a deep inward breath and slow down your pace. Do you lengthen in your body and feel stronger in your spine? Do you have a feeling of rebalancing and re-energizing?

Now practise the same exercise walking with your arms positioned as if you were riding. Take a deep inhalation and feel the stomach expand. Halt and feel the increased stability and power created in your strong abdominal centre. Then take a slow, long exhalation feeling the relaxation and fluidity run through your lower back. This energy flow is the key to absorbing forward movement.

Now repeat the breathing exercises and imagine how your hands, with closed fingers, can help to connect with the energy of the horse, contained through your lower back and strong centre. This is pivotal to the half halt; the energy is momentarily rebalanced and contained and then, on the outward breath, the energy is empowered and released into forward movement.

The relaxed lower back invites forward movement along with the allowing and opening of the fingers. The horse then accepts the invitation and takes the rebalanced energy forwards into a more elevated movement.

The combination of the half-halt and the subsequent release of the lower back and the opening of the fingers is the basis of riding in lightness.

The inward breath

Self-control in breathing helps to control the movement and balance of a horse. When a deep inward breath is taken, the forward energy flow is interrupted. The rider is rebalanced and poised, which in turn gives the signal to the horse to rebalance, i.e. to steady himself and engage his hindquarters. He will then take more of his body-weight back, thus lightening and elevating the forehand. This is the essence or 'spirit' of the half-halt; to rebalance the rider and to ask the horse to rebalance physically and focus and steady his mind (Figure 7.6).

The upper torso of the rider will lengthen and widen, allowing a holding or containing of energy. The pelvis is tipped very slightly forward and the seat bones move back. The lower back will arch, giving the indication to the horse to steady his forward movement.

The deep inhalation will influence the rider in the following ways.

- As air fills the lungs, it should be breathed into the back and spine. The hands placed on either side of the ribcage will feel the chest expand and widen, and the abdominal area will expand.
- The body is recharged with vital energy.
- The spine will strengthen and lengthen.
- The seat will lighten.

The deep inhalation should be followed by a slow exhalation from the lower abdomen.

7.6 Half-halt: the deep inward breath momentarily rebalances both horse and rider

The outward breath

Feel the deep exhalation send a ripple of energy down through the spine. Scoop up (draw upwards and inwards) the lower muscles of the stomach and pelvic floor, releasing and mobilizing the pelvis. (These are the muscles you can feel when you cough.) When these muscles are used correctly they will help to maintain core stability. This increased stability of the rider's back helps to maintain the quiet hand, giving fluidity and stability at the same time. The pelvis moves backwards as the seat bones move forwards and the lower back slightly flattens. The lower pelvic and transverse abdominal muscle tightens and gives a small 'push'. The horse will feel this release of energy which will encourage him to move forwards with an energetic flow (Figure 7.7). (Energy flow for the athlete is about flexibility and lack of any restriction. An awareness of breathing will help to achieve these goals for both horse and rider and help to reduce tension and stiffness.)

7.7 The outward breath: the horse feels the release of energy stimulating forward movement with lightness and balance

Maintain core stability

This does not mean that the horse is allowed to pull, but that the rider allows the horse to move forward, without restriction. Core stability is maintained.

The slow exhalation influences the rider in the following ways.

- A flow of energy through the upper body relaxes the ribcage.
- The lower spine is relaxed and softened, giving a feeling of 'melting' into the horse's back (Figure 7.8).
- The 'scoop' of the lower muscles of the pelvic floor can be felt when the stomach is hollowed.

Subtlety and sensitivity

If the horse does not respond to these sensitive aids, we will have to reinforce our commands with stronger body, hand and leg aids. If we continue to maintain the correct order of communication, very soon the horse *will* respond to the more sensitive aid. In this way he will learn to avoid the stronger leg and hand, and if we are coherent and consistent

7.8 Riding Maestu in trot with one hand on the reins. The rider's relaxed lower back, together with an allowing hand, encourages further balance and lightness

with our directions he will seek to please with the minimum of confrontation. We are responsible for the horse understanding our wishes, and constant repetition and encouragement is the path to success.

Once we have become aware of the techniques for breathing, the voyage of discovery of more subtle communication with a horse can begin. It is amazing how quickly a horse will tune in to a person's breathing. This should not come as a surprise because he is blessed with incredible sensitivity and an excellent memory.

We can use his extreme sensitivity to work for us. In the herd a horse is supremely sensitive to all the other herd members. There may be minor challenges of threatening behaviour within the herd, but the response is normally immediate and the friction is soon forgotten. They do not appear to seek major confrontation and seem content with their position, of whatever ranking, within the herd structure.

This type of behaviour tells us that if we seek minimal confrontation, we may succeed in gaining a positive response for much of the time to minimal aids.

There may be times when he does not listen so we will need to demonstrate our leadership more forcefully. We need to assert discipline but be quick with rewards and praise when the horse responds.

Have you ever been out walking on a windy day? There can appear a momentary peace and calmness where a feeling of quiet anticipation and stillness surrounds you. Suddenly the wind rushes in, swirling through the branches of trees and whistling over the hedges. The power of the wind can be intense but then slowly it recedes to a gentle breeze.

Breathing has similar traits; it can vary from the deeper more forceful breath to the barely perceived whisper. The wind can dramatically change the mood of a herd of horses from that of being totally relaxed to one of feeling apprehensive. The wind is an invisible force yet a source of great power. An awareness of breathing is a most powerful tool of communication. We can bring about telepathic responses, awakening a deeper connection with a horse.

Breathing the transitions
DOWNWARD TRANSITIONS
For a downward transition, rebalance your body with a deep inward

breath. The communication is the same as for the half-halt, but the rebalancing is taken a stage further, into the downward transition. The deep breath inwards will rebalance and steady the movement. Emphasize the deep breath and, as your strong centre 'balloons' forward, contain the energy in your hand. As the horse prepares for the downward transition, from trot into walk for example, allow your seat, back and breathing to emulate the walk rhythm.

If the horse does not respond, close your legs more on his sides and take more contact with the hands, using small vibrations of the wrist and fingers.

If the aids are always given in this sequence, where the breathing is used before any stronger aids, the horse will soon tune in and become more responsive. If he learns to respond to less, then frequently we will not have to ask with more!

UPWARD TRANSITIONS

Take the deeper breath inwards to prepare and then exhale fully into the abdomen and feel the release in the pelvis. The horse should learn to move forward from just this release of energy. If there is no response from the horse, use your legs on the girth with a tap, tap of the lower legs, and use the whip to support the legs if necessary.

When a rider's legs are used strongly it disrupts his balance, so a tap with the whip will be more effective and will help the rider to maintain stability.

The whip is to be used solely for encouragement and not to bully a horse. If he is unresponsive or lazy, a short, sharp tap with the whip may be necessary.

The horse will soon learn to respond to the first request for a transition, i.e. the exhalation, and will move up into the next gait once he understands this more natural method of communication.

Case Study: Teaching Carla

I was introduced to a substantial bay six-year-old warmblood mare. Carla had been brought on quite quickly by an experienced show-jumper and was bought by a young teenager who wanted her for competitive dressage and eventing. She had chosen her for her very kind, sweet nature and her enormous gaits. Good gaits should have not only forward movement, but also elevation and a potential for 'uphill' movement, particularly for the more advanced training.

I watched Carla for a while and she seemed to be taking a strong contact and not responding to her rider. She seemed very tense, almost too eager to please and over-anxious, which I think was a result of being brought on too quickly.

I then rode the mare to experience the feel she was offering and I talked through my techniques of breathing with her rider; she was extremely enthusiastic and agreed that I should try these concepts with Carla.

I began by halting, then I gave a deep breath outwards to ask her to walk forwards. She did not respond because, at this stage, my aids were too subtle and she expected more, and so I tapped her with my legs and she walked on. She was full of energy, rushing and pulling at my arms. I wanted her to work forwards but I was also trying to ask her to listen and wait, thus calming her mind.

I worked her on a circle initially to encourage her to take the outside rein contact correctly and to work away from my inside leg and hand. She was leaning her weight to the inside of the circle and was not equally balanced. I tried to focus her energy for several minutes and when the walk felt more steady and relaxed I asked for trot using my deep, outward breath. Carla walked a little faster, which was good as she was now listening to me. I praised her for the response and breathed outwards again. She then moved forward into a good trot rhythm. She felt the increased mobility in my seat created by the deep outward breath. Being a very sensitive mare she responded with more energy. I tried to breathe in accord with her rhythm and Carla's back gradually began to lift and relax. My steady breathing was reflected in the relaxation throughout my body and Carla's demeanour became more relaxed and her strides more fluid as she became more attentive to my communication.

Breathing reflects the state of mind

Carla needed to take more weight by engaging her inside hind and so I repositioned my upper body slightly, bringing my left shoulder back a fraction, thus releasing my left upper thigh. This allowed Carla to feel my softer position and to further engage her inside hind but I had to control her effectively with my outside leg and hand to prevent her quarters swinging out from the correct path of the circle.

As the lesson continued, Carla slowly began to calm down, she listened to me less anxiously and she took a more relaxed contact with my hand. When I felt the time was right, I asked Carla's owner if she would like to ride Carla and feel the changes in her attitude. Her initial feeling was that the mare was more relaxed in her neck and back and she was more accepting of a steady contact with the hand.

She also felt a more positive, steady rhythm from her mare, who was showing a calmer attitude and a greater ability to wait for instruction. Together they began to experience the feeling of tuning in to each other's thoughts.

Looking at our Communication

We can learn to become thinking riders if we begin to assess why we use different ways of communicating with the horse. Have you ever felt the weight of a rucksack or a child carried on your back? The slightest movement has a disruptive impact on your ability to carry the weight and the smallest movement can displace all feeling of balance.

When we close our legs on a horse and use more physical force with our body we are having a disrupting effect upon his balance. If he is capable of understanding and responding to less, why do more?

During a training session, there will be moments of extra tension: perhaps a horse has not listened to you and takes time to accept your leadership and discipline or it may be that the training has demanded more in-depth concentration on a certain aspect of the work. For instance, we may be teaching the horse a different movement in which he has to balance himself differently and adjust to new aids. When a rider has become self-aware and is observant of when a horse becomes tense, it is possible to become more effective by the use of lighter aids and to respond to his tension and mood with breathing techniques to help him relax his mind and become calmer. In this way he will be able to perform new movements with more fluidity and concentration.

There may be a moment when we realize that excess stress has built up and the horse is trying too hard, resulting in him becoming too 'tight' or apprehensive. This could be the moment to reward the generosity of the horse with a relaxed walk on a loose rein. A deep sigh from the rider and a stroke of the horse's neck can encourage the horse to let go of his built-up anxiety. He will sense the relaxation of the

7.9 Keep the aids subtle and easily understood

rider and release his tension more easily. This is the best way forward for our training; both horse and rider can return to their work feeling fresh and relaxed both physically and mentally.

My time spent teaching Spanish Pure-breds has taught me that they will resist strong aids and I have to continually reassess communication to keep the aids subtle and easily understood (Figure 7.9).

The breathing techniques can be used in furthering lateral work and teaching advanced movements (later chapters will discuss these concepts in relation to riding shoulder-in, half-pass and more advanced exercises). We are allowing the horse to travel forwards more freely if we can use less force, and correct breathing reduces our own stress levels and helps us to focus and develop concentration.

The Competition Rider

Breathing: the golden tool

It is now common practice for competitive riders to employ sports psychologists to help them cope with the more stressful environment of the competition arena.

Some riders find competition stimulating; others may feel that competition is necessary to prove the progress of their training. All this addresses the needs and feelings of the rider but the horse has to find his own level of tolerance when on the competition circuit.

Our breathing techniques, however, can really benefit not only the rider but also the horse. The deeper awareness and practice of this way of breathing will immediately help a rider to become more at one with his horse. In the potentially over-exciting atmosphere of a competition, the steady breathing of a horse's 'herd leader' will transmit calm to the horse, help him to relax, work with, and to listen to, his rider more effectively and to concentrate on the rider's aids.

Teach your horse to listen

A rider will find this communication invaluable when warming up for a competition and when riding the dressage test itself. At a competition, it is difficult to attain the same quality of communication as can be achieved at home when working quietly with few distractions.

These techniques should help both horse and rider to keep relaxed and focused on their work. The aim of competition is to demonstrate the level of training achieved in the partnership of both horse and rider. The judge will be looking for harmonious, invisible aids and the application of these techniques can produce a more artistic combination of horse and rider, working together, as one.

Relationships between people may be harmonious under normal circumstances but strain can appear if the stresses of life become too much; it then takes more effort to listen and communicate, which is also true of relationships with horses. It is not only important that you listen to your horse, but also that he should wish to listen to you and look to you for guidance and leadership, particularly in tension-inducing situations, such as competitions and shows. At a competition, the horse will be aware of the body language and breathing of his rider, even if the individual is totally oblivious to the signals he is giving.

To ensure that your horse listens and responds to you at competitions and shows, when he could be more easily influenced by other stimuli, you must start to build the correct relationship early on. Loose work together with a wide use of breathing techniques and body language can change the way a horse views his relationship with a rider and can build the bond of trust required (Figure 7.10).

7.10 Delfin and Jenny building a bond of trust through loose work

This trust and respect is something that a client of mine was not given by her competition horse. He was a strong-minded warmblood horse and she felt he was becoming too dominant. The problems began with the ground work; he was forceful with his body language and lacked respect for his handler. His attitude to their relationship was taken into the ridden work and thus the battle for supremacy became fraught with problems for the rider. This lack of respect dominated the whole relationship which was presented with some tough encounters during the ridden work.

Initially, when I suggested that time was spent working the horse loose, my client looked rather surprised as, in her experience, any confrontation in ridden work during training was addressed under saddle. After some sessions of loose work, however, the horse began to show my client more respect because she began to understand how to become the leader in the relationship.

When ridden work was recommenced, my client addressed the many small issues of dominance as they happened because she was more aware of his code of behaviour.

He was not, for example, allowed just to walk off as she mounted. If he became resistant to her leadership, she would calmly persevere with winning his co-operation. Her self-discipline began to reap rewards and her horse became more trusting and willing to listen.

I could see a transformation taking place where riding and competing became 'lighter' and more fun. A relationship of harmony was being built, which meant that both horse and rider could give of their best in a calmer frame of mind. Together they were regularly placed and gained numerous awards in both dressage and eventing.

In the Classical Tradition

The art of classical training is to try to find invisible, harmonious techniques to use as a means of instruction for the horse. The classical rider will be seeking to attain a seat of stability, not by force, but by appearing to be effortless. When the rider is aware of the importance of breathing, the mind is focused and the body is energized, well prepared to move in balance with the horse. The upper torso should be in a natural self-carriage and the legs should hang long, be relaxed and stay close to the body of the horse. This posture will augment the classical seat, helping the horse and rider to move as one and, together with correct breathing, will assist them to share the same thoughts, rhythm and harmony, thus enhancing the unseen telepathy which exists in every close relationship.

Have you ever walked into a room where two people are standing in silence? The body language and atmosphere tell you instantly that there has been friction; no words are spoken but you are aware of tension all around you, but if you walk up to a group of friends who are smiling and radiating fun and friendship, the relaxed body language and smiles give a feeling that instantly lifts your spirits. Horses perceive these signals very easily and it is important that they consistently pick up the smiles, fun and friendship.

When you can experience the feeling of the horse responding to your breath, or just a deep sigh, there is a deep emotional response and understanding which can never be felt from a stronger, more abusive language of communication. If a horse is prepared to listen to such whispered instructions, a relationship rooted in the classical ideals of knowledge, respect, empathy and harmony will guarantee an exciting future when both man and horse will continue to listen to, and learn from, each other.

Learning creates knowledge — knowledge creates skill — skill creates empathy — empathy creates a true classical rider.

As a physiotherapist, Celia Cohen helps both riders and their horses obtain ultimate balance with maximum athletic ability and suppleness. She also endorses, and shares, my feelings about the importance of breathing techniques in riding and training, something she describes here.

'Jenny has taught me that a mixture of art, love and intuition is required when training a horse and rider, and the significance of the vital body-and-mind state of the rider and how to achieve this through breathing techniques. At first glance this might seem either obvious or too alternative, but Jenny tries to convey the message by guiding a student away from the traditional aid/action and towards the use of "feel" and inner strength from which directing a horse's movement becomes "quieter" and "simpler".

'As a trainer she demonstrates the importance of understanding and patience, looking always for the true ability within each horse. All horses are capable of demonstrating their unique beauty in their natural movement and dressage should not be about falsifying this but facilitating it.

'Is this not true horsemanship and training?'

Warming up: taking the time to focus and listen (photo: Barrie Rolfe)

Chapter Eight

Warming Up Under Saddle

'Let us use our wisdom as we seek to understand the horse'
Jenny Rolfe

Successful warming up is an art that will evolve slowly with dedication and practice. Always listen to your horse; he will be your greatest influence.

Any exercise, whether for human or horse, requires that muscles are warmed up and loosened before work can begin. Only the muscles which have been allowed sufficient time to warm up, will be capable of stretching sufficiently, to protect the joints during exercise. Cold weather or stress can tighten these muscles. Injury, stiffness and pain may be caused if these concepts are not fully understood.

If you work-out at a gymnasium you will perform exercises that prepare you for the more strenuous athletic movements. In my experience, you are initially taught to control your breathing and then work through some gentle, stretching exercises in rhythm with your deeper inhalation and exhalation. When the body is feeling more relaxed and mobilized then more ambitious exercises can commence.

The time we allow for effectively warming up a horse will ensure that the training session can progress with more empathy and less resistance. The time can be used to settle the horse into his work and to get his muscles working in a fluid and supple way. If the warm-up period is not rushed and forced, the more demanding work later in the session will be easier and more harmonious.

Should a rider not understand the purpose of warming up, the work will lack inspiration and improvement and if this persists it will prevent the horse's training from progressing with any consistency. A horse will continue to work in the same way at the same level unless we concentrate on exercises that can improve his athletic ability.

It is important that the warming-up period should not only be targeted towards the physical requirements of the horse but also his mental requirements and attitude. Without a work ethos, the horse may lack concentration and energy and it is the responsibility of the rider to provide the structure of training where this will be achieved.

A focus on breathing enhances concentration

Training cannot progress with a lack of submission or inadequate energy. When the work moves on to the more advanced movements, a dearth of time spent in basic work may cause problems to arise. The aim is to achieve looseness, rhythm and straightness in all three gaits, with a submissive and attentive attitude from our horse.

A trainer should try to instil a desire for active, energetic forward movement in the horse; it is not good that he has to be continually asked for this; always having to push a horse is disruptive to riding.

The loose work and lungeing should already have initiated a more athletic attitude in the horse as, unless there is sufficient energy, the horse cannot work correctly through his back to relax through the poll. Although physically the energy is being produced by the hind limbs, the source of the energy is rooted in the horse's mind, thus, in order to achieve positive forward gaits, his mind must be motivated as well.

Horses enjoy movement: mares and youngstock in particular love to chase each other in the field, playing, galloping and developing new games, just for the sheer joy of expressing their freedom in movement

8.1 A horse enjoying freedom of movement

(Figure 8.1). The art for the classical rider is the ability to introduce discipline without sacrificing enjoyment for either the horse or rider. Throughout training we are trying to give the horse an opportunity to reveal his personality and exuberance within his work.

Imagine a child at school sitting in a classroom; he may be full of vitality and fun and focused on the distractions of the world outside the classroom window. A strict, inflexible teacher may initially challenge the mind of the child but it will take an understanding and perceptive teacher with enthusiasm and a feel for his subject to gain and maintain his pupil's interest. If a teacher can stimulate the child's imagination, he might even be able to imbue the pupil with a passion for a particular subject.

The equine pupil will react in the same way. There is often no middle ground, he will either have his attention wholly on his trainer or be totally distracted. It will be impossible to produce any work of artistic value unless a horse is part of the life and vitality of the whole picture.

Everyone can use a tap of the whip to ask the horse to focus on the

The
enthusiastic
rider
produces
alert,
responsive
horses

rider, but what happens after that? It might be necessary to reprimand an inattentive horse but this action needs to be followed by appropriate praise when he begins to respond in a more positive manner. The trainer's encouragement will gain his confidence and a willingness to please.

I have heard riders say that training can become boring but have met others for whom training horses is a passion. A horse will not find enthusiasm for his work unless the rider is stimulated by and enthusiastic about both the schooling and his partnership with a horse. This is where an understanding of breathing techniques can become influential. When such subtle communication inspires a horse to concentrate more fully on his rider, they move in total harmony with each other, their minds become as one and a passion for the work develops.

Goals for Warming Up

* To ask the horse to listen to our thoughts.
* To give the horse an opportunity to work with looseness and an absence of tension – the German term for this is *losgelassenheit* (Figure 8.2).
* To achieve a good natural rhythm in each gait.
* To gain an obedient and cooperative attitude.
* To encourage long and low work (see page 174).
* To help both horse and rider to work in natural balance.
* To use exercises in the school to achieve these goals.

Focus on the Horse

If the horse has been standing in the stable for a long period, he will need some time to release the stiffness and tightness within his muscles. He will then feel comfortable and relaxed for the more demanding exercises later in the session. There is a possibility that he could be feeling a little sore from the previous day's work or that he has, perhaps, slept in an uncomfortable position the previous night. Equally, there may be a feeling of anxiety or lethargy. The warm-up period should be used to study his frame of mind as our observations can influence the methods and exercises used later in the schooling session. For this reason warming up the horse from the ground can be so effective; his gaits and facial expressions can be more easily seen.

8.2 Jenny is encouraging Delfin to take the contact forwards and down by offering a relaxed contact from a loose rein

If the warm-up is carried out under saddle, the first few minutes would be well spent just walking on a loose rein when the horse can start to focus on the work and his muscles will begin to loosen up. He will also look around and take in any changes in his surroundings. He will gain confidence if the rider sits quietly, taking the time to relax and become self-aware and to allow his body and mind to link up with that of the horse.

From calmness comes positive energy

I would recommend a period of time warming up in the basic forward gaits, either on the lunge or under saddle before beginning any lateral exercises. During the first few minutes of riding, keep the reins longer and ride frequent transitions from walk to trot and trot to canter, and then come back through the downward transitions. Ride on both reins equally to warm up the horse's muscles and to help him to become more obedient, relaxed and supple.

The rider needs to think about lightness and self-carriage and if the horse attempts to dominate by pulling, the deeper inward breath, which supports the rider's back, will assist in steadying the pace. If the horse does not respond and continues to forge ahead, the rider will have to use

8.3 Using the forward seat to redistribute the rider's weight

a stronger vibration of the hand and wrist. Timing is so important and as soon as the horse rebalances and responds with submission to the rider, the pressure of the hand can revert to an allowing hand.

If the horse is very lively, work in a slightly faster gait for a few moments, as long as he is not pulling. Thus excess energy can be released and after a while he can be asked to work in a steadier rhythm.

During the canter work the rider can use the forward seat which will redistribute the weight of the rider, taking pressure away from the horse's spine (Figure 8.3). In this way the horse has the opportunity to warm up effectively. If he is allowed to move freely through his back, this will enhance elevation and increase his athletic mobility.

If the horse continues to try to dominate by forging ahead and evading your commands, bring him back to walk because he can be more easily controlled in this gait and you can re-establish his submission and your leadership. If he then takes a good steady contact when he is ridden forward into trot again, reward him with your voice and the lightest of aids. As you progress in trot, should he attempt to take over again and pull, quickly take a deeper breath inwards and bring him back into walk. He will soon learn that you do not allow him to pull you around the arena.

Frequent transitions on a circle are also helpful in addressing this dominance problem and, equally, the laid-back horse can be encouraged to become more lively and responsive by using the upward transitions to gain more energy and impulsion.

Once the horse becomes submissive to the closed fingers, allow a more giving contact and 'play' the fingers very lightly. Imagine holding a bird with delicate feathers in your hand; the contact must keep the bird from flying away but not damage the wings. This is the delicate contact the horse should feel in his mouth when he has become responsive to our hands.

During any conversation there will be a time for listening and a time for talking, a time for reinforcement and a time to ease up. This is the essence of a conversation with a horse; the contact will include all of these concepts plus wisdom, feel and timing.

My methods do not seek to pull the horse into an outline; the words of Nuno Oliveira, 'the hands belong to the horse' should always be remembered. The horse should be persuaded forward on a long rein and gradually to work in a long and low outline. The feel should be an elastic one, a mutual 'giving' between the horse and the rider's hands, when he is not 'pulling' at the hands or bearing down with his head and neck. If breathing techniques are used to rebalance the horse, he will find it more difficult to place his head and neck in a position from which it is easy to bear down.

When the horse attempts to disregard instructions, there are exercises that can be utilized to gain his cooperation and ensure that he is working correctly from the diagonal aids. The goals of the basic work are relaxed yet rhythmic and energetic gaits, a longer deeper outline, which allows the back muscles to gently stretch from the tail through to the neck and poll. We should encourage fluidity with straightness and submission in the work. The contact must allow the horse to find his own balance, self-carriage and stability; allowing hands permit a horse to take his energy forward and guide him towards his own natural balance. In every upward transition, walk into trot for example, the hand must yield to the forward movement. True balance and natural carriage can never be achieved if the horse meets resistance from restricting hands; the strong contact will

> Guide the horse to seek his own self-carriage

make the horse start to look to the hand for support and he will become dependent on the rider to carry the weight of his forehand.

Exercises for Warming Up

Antonio Borba Monteiro taught me a very important exercise on a circle, which helps a horse to take the correct contact into the outside rein. To ride this exercise, walk on a 15 m or 20 m circle, then turn your shoulders and upper torso slightly to the inside of the circle. With your inside leg placed slightly behind the girth, ask the horse to move his quarters away from your inside leg and towards your outside hand and leg; the outside leg will support and contain the movement. The outside rein is both the receiving and supporting rein. The inside rein will ask for the inside flexion and allow a giving contact when the horse has yielded and relaxed into the movement. The neck should be flexed away from the direction of the movement, i.e. if the movement is to the right, the neck flexion is to the left. (Figures 8.4 and 8.5a–d.) Perform this exercise for just a few strides. Feel the horse working into the outside rein and moving away from your inside hand and leg. Focusing on your breathing will enable you to allow your seat to absorb the sideways motion of the horse more freely. Your shoulders will help to guide the movement of the horse. The inside hand (wrist) should be turned slightly inwards (towards the rider's abdomen) when positioning

Ask, wait, receive and give

the neck of the horse. The flexion to the inside is asked for with a squeezing of the fingers. A constant connection is not required; we ask, and wait for, the flexion and when we receive it, we give by relaxing the fingers. This will guide the horse to working correctly into the outside rein contact, using the basic principles of the diagonal aids. Bring the horse back onto the circle again and continue to walk forwards.

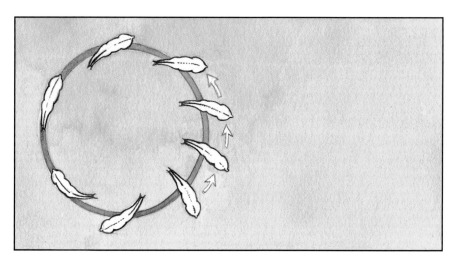

8.4 Exercise for warming up on the circle.

a

b

c

d

8.5a-d a) Ask the horse to move his quarters away from your inside leg (rear view); b) Ask the horse to move his quarters away from your inside leg (front view); c) Working into the outside rein and moving away from your inside hand and leg (rear view); d) Working into the outside rein and moving away from your inside hand and leg (front view)

When this submission is established, take a deep breath inwards and then on the outward breath ride forwards into an energetic trot, using the whip to reinforce the aids if he is lazy and does not respond immediately. Maintain the contact into the outside rein and leg allowing the horse to work forwards and into a longer, lower frame. Ask the horse to stretch forward and down in the trot work. This is a valuable stretching exercise for the horse because he lengthens his spine and neck towards his natural 'grazing position'. Some horses have the ability to stretch more than others and this exercise should *never* be forced but should just allow and encourage the forward-downward stretch. The lateral exercises in walk are executed with a normal length of rein; only when working forwards in trot does the rider give a greater length of rein to encourage the longer, lower outline (Figure 8.6).

8.6 When working forwards in trot, lengthen the reins to encourage the longer, lower outline

If at any stage the horse falls back heavily against your inside aids, repeat the exercise on the circle in walk until he again submits to the diagonal aids and works into the outside hand and leg. It is easier for a horse to understand what is required if we stop the exercise as soon as things go wrong. When all is going smoothly, however, the good work should be praised and encouraged and not be interfered with. When you ride forwards into trot again, allow a longer rein to permit the horse to lengthen and lift his spine and work with fluidity and submission.

Exercises to supple and strengthen

During this warm-up period, good forward-moving gaits have been encouraged together with the exercise on the circle in order to help establish the correct contact.

If a horse is naturally supple and can move with fluidity in lateral work, it may be constructive to progress by focusing on his basic forward movement. Some horses are naturally supple and move easily into lateral movements. Time has to be spent with this type of horse to develop the forward gaits and straightness. Other horses may be moving forward well with energetic gaits and so, after working in this way for a few minutes, the use of steady, lateral exercises in walk will help to build more suppleness. This structured work helps to build up the muscles slowly over a period of time, and will support the horse in his more advanced work.

The lateral work develops lightness by inducing the correct engagement of the hind limbs and stimulating freedom and elasticity in the shoulders. Always start these exercises in walk until you feel that the horse can be placed in any direction with a greater feel of suppleness and mobility.

SHOULDER-IN

The correct preparation for this movement is the key to success, and so start by asking the horse to walk forwards slowly but with energy and submission. The energy is important as you want to begin with a responsive but submissive horse.

When working on the left rein, as you leave the short side to travel up the long side of the school, ride a 10 m circle in the corner (Figure 8.7). On returning to the long side continue riding up the long side and position the forehand and shoulders of the horse to face the diagonal line. Prepare to take a stride across the diagonal then instigate a half-halt with a deeper inward breath. Control the position of the horse with your right hand and leg. Use your inside (left) hand to promote flexion and when the horse relaxes his head and neck into the correct flexion (away from the dirrection of travel) release your fingers with an 'allowing' contact. Then take a deeper outward breath which will bring about a released energy flow through your lower back. Your inside (left) leg will ask the horse to move the inside hind leg both forwards and laterally. Your relaxed spine will enable the horse to move more freely, elevating his back through the lateral excercise. Ensure you are sitting centrally within the movement so that you can support the horse with both your balance and breathing (Figures 8.8a and b).

Ride several strides of shoulder-in up the long side and then reposition and continue walking straight ahead.

The shoulder-in exercise can be executed using three or four tracks and both are beneficial in all stages of training to enhance lightness and mobility of the shoulders.

TRAVERS (HAUNCHES IN)

When you have straightened the horse after shoulder-in, walk for a short distance and then prepare for travers. It can also be effective to ride shoulder-in in walk to the corner of the school and use the bend of the school to help you change to travers (Figure 8.9). Steady and control the front of the horse with both reins to keep him straight and keep his shoulders on the track. Your inside leg on the girth will maintain or create impulsion along with your seat and breathing. Position your outside shoulder and outside leg slightly back to encourage the horse's outside hind leg to take an inside track. As with shoulder-in, continue to use your breathing to maintain balance within the movement. This mobilizes your lower back so that there is no resistance to the horse's movement. Just ride a few steps of this movement and then straighten the horse to walk forwards again on the track. (Figure 8.10.)

8.7 A 10 m circle is a good preparation for the shoulder-in

a   b

8.8a and b a) Maestu: three-track shoulder-in on the right rein and b) four-track shoulder-in on the left rein

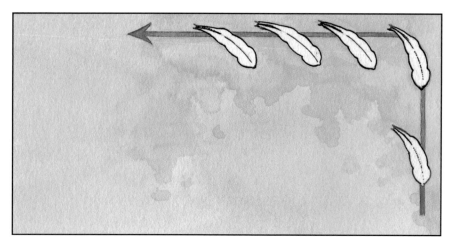

8.9 Shoulder-in to the corner then a change to travers

8.10 Travers on the right rein

Thoughtful preparation, the key to correct movements

This exercise can also be performed on a circle by asking for just a few strides of travers and then refreshing with a forward walk.

When he begins to understand these exercises, your aids can become more subtle.

Once the shoulder-in and travers are established, they can become the preparation for riding the half-pass.

As a result of these steady lateral exercises, a horse should begin to feel really submissive, more springy and collected. Impulsion is not just about forward movement but also upward lift and cadence, i.e. time spent in balanced suspension. The horse's weight distribution will alter as the hind limbs engage more and are able to propel the horse forwards more efficiently, which, in turn, gives an added lightness, grace and elevation to the forehand. Correctly spaced trotting poles can assist the horse to elevate and move in a steadier, more balanced way (see page 183).

During a teaching session I regularly reward the horse for good work by riding at walk on a loose rein and stroking his neck. The horse appreciates the freedom from the aids and considers this to be a reward. I also give a deep sigh which the horse copies and this allows him to release any built-up tension, and to relax his ribcage and whole body. A horse needs to be breathing with both relaxation and rhythm to be able to work correctly.

It is important that you ride all these exercises initially for only a few strides before riding forward and straight again. The lateral work will help to supple the horse, but always refresh with energetic forward strides to reactivate the horse physically and mentally. If when you ride forward on a loose rein the horse reaches forward and down, stretching and relaxing his neck, the work has been beneficial (Figure 8.11).

Walk on a loose rein during the warm-up

8.11 The work has proved to be beneficial when the horse stretches forward and down when given a loose rein

Important guidelines for lateral exercises

- **Prepare well** before the exercise.
- Keep the walk **steady** but **energetic**.
- After **lateral exercises**, refresh the work by **riding forward and straight**.
- **Reward often** by riding on a **loose rein** at walk.
- Aim to work your horses in **balance** and **lightness**.

Working Towards Harmony

Let us look at some problems that might occur during the warm-up part of a training session. A horse might walk round on a loose rein quite happily but immediately a contact is taken up, resistance and tension is felt. You may find that a horse feels energetic and spooky, or he might decide to set his jaw and neck muscles and try to forge ahead. There are ways to address these difficulties and so we will look at some techniques and exercises that may be helpful.

Use your mind to avoid confrontation

If a horse is feeling particularly over-exuberant and behaving in a high-spirited manner, the idea is to use logic to help gain his attention and make him concentrate, whilst avoiding confrontation.

You may choose to start work on a circle and then wish to continue by using the whole school. If, as you go large, the horse decides to look around him and lose concentration, one method is to ask for a shoulder-in 'feel' for a few strides. This is the feel of lightening the inside shoulder and positioning it slightly to the inside of the track, with the horse showing a good relaxed inside neck flexion. It is not ridden as a specific three- or four-track exercise, although the result may be the same, but it makes it difficult for the horse to bring his head up and look around. Insist that he maintains this flexion to the inside with the feeling of shoulder-in. When he submits to your aids, allow the fingers of your inside hand to relax and continue round the school with the horse again working correctly towards the outside hand and leg.

You may, for example, be approaching a corner that the horse finds particularly spooky and from which he backs off and threatens not to go forwards. Try circling away from the track in a 10 m or 15 m circle, depending on the suppleness of your horse, and when you arrive back on the track reposition into a shoulder-in feel again and progress forwards, being prepared for another similar circle exercise if necessary. This way of riding gives the horse something to occupy his mind; continuing to work in a straight line towards a spooky corner will give him time to think of an evasion.

After working in this way for several minutes, you will probably find that his attitude changes and you will be able to work forwards in a straight line with a more relaxed horse. When you encourage forward energy it will reinforce your leadership but if you allow the gait to deteriorate and the horse to back off then he will start to dominate you.

An alternative technique for calming a horse and gaining his attention in a place he considers unsettling, is to walk up to it, ask for halt and then concentrate on relaxed breathing, and even yawning. If the horse responds by relaxing his neck and back, reward him with a longer rein and stroke his neck before walking on again with him in a calmer frame of mind. This spot in the school then becomes a place for harmony rather than fear.

It is possible to discipline a horse without being angry. A well-timed tap with the whip can bring a quick response from a horse but if he feels your frustration he will become tense and resist your aids. How many of us have been in this no-win situation?

If a horse is resisting because of tension, to respond with very strong aids will induce further aggravation. This type of relationship evolves in the same way as a couple of people shouting, with frustration, to get their point across; neither person is really listening to the other. In a case like this, a rider needs to make the horse feel that he is on the horse's side and that he is grateful for the horse's generosity; it is wrong to impose dominance in every situation.

> Our thinking power, not our physical power, allows us to work more sympathetically with a horse

The art of finding a solution to this type of problem is to take a moment to breathe, and to regain balance, mentally and physically, and positive communication. It will always be our thinking power and *not* our physical power that allows us to work more sympathetically with a horse.

When warming up, try to settle a horse if he is rushing, or create more energy if he is being lazy. Riding frequent transitions will help to make the horse more attentive and enhance both balance and engagement, thus achieving more lightness. Training is about finding ways to ask a horse to work with you and if he begins to listen in the warm-up phase it is more likely he will continue to work with you during the remainder of a training session. Remember, dancing partners are in tune with each other and the best dancers share a flow of harmony, energy and rhythm.

Trotting Poles

I regularly use trotting poles during a warm-up session. As has been proven when the horse is on the lunge, these exercises help the horse to

8.12 Trotting poles can be useful when warming up under saddle; Celia riding Maestu

concentrate more on his work and help him to be more aware of himself and his limbs and where he is placing his feet (Figure 8.12).

If a lazy horse has to focus his attention on a series of trotting poles, his work might become more animated. Several poles should be placed either in a straight line or on a circle, spaced at the correct distance for the natural stride of the individual horse.

If a horse has a naturally long stride that propels him forwards out of his natural balance, carefully placed trotting poles can help to regulate his stride and if the poles are raised a few inches above the ground, the horse then begins to develop suspension and flexion within his joints.

Working steadily, i.e. without rushing, whilst practising these exercises will help the horse to gain activity, not just with forward movement but also with cadence and elevation. He will begin to lift his back, which will instigate the correct use of his muscles. This is of fundamental importance to a horse if he is to gain the physical ability required to progress in his training.

The use of poles will encourage the horse to think ahead and focus, working with an energetic swing in his stride. This will help to create a stronger natural rhythm thus enhancing both balance and self-carriage.

The art of successful warming up will develop with dedication and practice.

At the end of every training session, the horse should be ridden calmly on a loose rein, thus allowing him to stretch and relax the muscles he has been working. He should have a relaxed and contented facial expression and eyes with alert twitching ears, relaxed nostrils and a moist mouth with a relaxed jaw gently chomping on the bit.

The most important lesson will always be to listen to the horse. He is our greatest teacher.

Roberto Novoa riding Quimico (photo: Rafael Lemos)

Chapter Nine

Building on Strong Foundations

Building friendship creates a place of safety and peace where minds can think as one.
Jenny Rolfe

I n the Bible there is a parable about a wise man and a foolish man who both build a house, one on sand and the other on rocks. The weather lashed against the house on the sand and it crumbled beneath the pressure of the elements. The house founded on the solid rock stood firm against the destructive storms. This parable encouraged the followers of Jesus to build firm foundations for their faith.

Building firm foundations applies to many aspects of our lives including the training of horses. We all hope that the many hours spent with our horses will enhance our understanding of them and that this will be quite evident to anyone observing our partnerships. Strong training foundations should be the same for all horses, no matter what their potential field, and will benefit them both mentally and physically. Dressage, for example, is not just about performing isolated individual movements in the school; all the movements must be developed and built upon in a logical progression of horsemanship to form a harmonious whole.

Everyone who paints a picture or carves a piece of wood is seeking to mould something that is inspired by the heart and it will take all of their sensitivity and patience to achieve it. The path to creating art is not easily defined in academic terms because it requires not only a practical ability but can also have a spiritual aspect, demanding everything that is creative to be continuously reborn. Art evolves as we apply a creative element to training, not just on one particular day but every day. The challenge is to aspire to giving of our most creative nature during the course of training, which demands dedication. It is much 'easier' to give less.

For example, if a horse performs half-pass in a tense, stiff and uncooperative way, this may tell us that the horse is momentarily uneasy or that his training has maybe been rushed and not carried out in a thoughtful manner. A horse needs to feel confident mentally and physically for the movements to flow, and therein lies the art.

> Routine provides the repetition that becomes the foundation for learning

The daily routine of improving basic gaits is fundamental to our training goals; the routine provides the repetition, which becomes the basis for learning.

Following a Logical Progression

Daily observation and acknowledgement of the small problems will pave the way to training on solid foundations. There may be days when a horse can cope willingly with new work and be mentally in accord with his rider; on other days it may be better to work for a short period on lessons already learnt and understood. The ability to judge the horse's mood on the day can help people to become good trainers and be aware of their own limitations.

Problems which might occur during training can be caused by a lack of preparation and this may be apparent in the quality of the basic work. For instance, flying changes require a horse's hindquarters to be truly engaged with sufficient 'jump' in the stride and must also be balanced and straight. This quality of movement can only be produced after hours of practice when the understanding between horse and rider is fully developed. Also, the strength and flexibility in the horse must have been built up gradually in order to create sufficient power from the hindquarters. Once the muscles of the hindquarters have been developed, the horse will work with increased strength and this will alter his balance. When the horse has sufficient power and cadence, he can begin to work in greater self-carriage: the weight distribution will be taken more by the hindquarters allowing more freedom and elevation of the shoulders, and the gaits will be more expressive and will enhance the feeling for the rider of dancing with the horse in lightness (Figure 9.1).

9.1 Ignacio Ramblas dancing with his horse

If the horse has been carefully brought on in this way with loose work, followed by lunge work and work in-hand, a good grounding has already been achieved. My teaching, inspired by the Portuguese classical training methods, will help to prepare a horse efficiently to progress through the stages of basic training. These stages are known as training scales; they form a logical and progressive sequence and are used as training guidelines amongst horsemen in Germany, the U.K. and other European countries.

The training scales
- *Losgelassenheit* (looseness and freedom in the gaits)
- Rhythm
- Contact
- *Schwung* (the ability to move with elasticity and 'swing' produced from the energy from the hind limbs; the gaits look expressive and have vigour)
- Straightness
- Collection

LOSGELASSENHEIT

A lack of tension and a supple body, 'freedom within movement', are prerequisites for a horse's more advanced training.

To achieve loose and supple gaits, a horse has to feel confident and relaxed; his work can then benefit from vibrant and positive energy (Figure 9.2). The aim is to help a horse build upon his basic desire for movement; lungeing, work in-hand and ridden exercises in the school will all help, and the use of trotting poles and gymnastic jumping exercises will help the horse to gain impulsion and elasticity, together with more confidence and interest in his work.

Horses being trained at a more advanced level will always benefit from time spent working on the basic principles of dressage: looseness, a calmness in the work, energy, straightness, obedience and submission, which will always be the key to improving the more advanced movements.

9.2 When a horse is confident and relaxed, his work can benefit from vibrant and positive energy

RHYTHM

Progression in training leads to more cadence within the natural rhythm which will vary from horse to horse. Rhythm is essential to dressage and nature has given some horses a greater ability and talent for performing with a regular tempo (rate) and beat than others. Rhythm will improve with training as the horse gains in flexibility and power.

The rhythm of the gait should carry the horse forwards in balance but it may take some time to gain good stability when the horse is overexcited and rushes his strides. If a horse is feeling either high-spirited or anxious, a trainer should try to produce a calmer energy. He needs to gain confidence, so that it gives him pleasure to work for his trainer and tune into his thoughts and requests. He will be able to learn more quickly if his mind can be calmed. Basic work in walk and trot transitions will help to steady him especially if it is carried out with quiet voice and aids.

Lazy gaits need to be encouraged to become more springy and full of vitality. In fact, if I am lungeing a lazy-minded horse, I do initially encourage him to work with more activity, sometimes out of his natural rhythm. This serves to activate his mind and wake him up so that he starts to move with purpose and energy. When he readily moves forward in his stride, then I allow him to work in a slower, more natural rhythm. Impulsion is necessary to produce good rhythm and contact in training.

Once a horse has learnt to support his weight, together with that of a rider, in a balanced way, then the rhythm will become more established and he will carry himself upwards as well as forwards. The energy and power from the hindquarters will begin to elevate the forehand, which will enhance the natural balance of the gaits. This connection of power and submission will help to establish better rhythm.

CONTACT

This part of training requires time and patience in order to build up a horse's necessary confidence. If a horse trots about with his head in the air, looking all around him, there is no positive connection emotionally or physically with the rider. When two people are talking, if one is trying to maintain a conversation, whilst the other is distracted by children playing or noises coming from another room, there is no communication. Communication takes two: one to talk and one to listen and both should be prepared to change the sequence, allowing the other person to contribute to the conversation.

Contact is the way a rider converses with a horse; a good contact, therefore, is when the rider is having a conversation with the horse during which neither becomes dominant. A horse has to be willing to take up an elastic contact with his rider's hands without forging ahead and pulling. When a rider rebalances himself and takes a deeper inward breath, the horse should steady his gait to absorb the altered balance of the rider and thus lighten the contact. The rider then uses the lightened contact to allow the horse to work in self-carriage.

Contact is also a connection with the horse's mind

It is important to remember that contact is established, not only with the head and mouth of the horse, but also with his mind.

Thoughts on contact

A conversation or connection between two living beings requires:

- a time to listen
- a time to express thoughts or requests
- the creation of a rapport or dialogue: information being both offered and received
- a mutual desire to understand the feelings of the other party.

The head connection

When a horse is moving freely, the first part of his body to make a move forward is his head. If, however, a rider restricts this forward movement with heavy hands, this restriction will act like a brake, physically and mentally, and will only serve to discourage the horse from enjoying the forward movement. Confusion will ensue if a rider uses his seat and legs to ask for forward movement and then creates a barrier against it with the hands; the result will be an anxious and frustrated horse.

It is essential that our hands allow the unrestricted motion of the horse's head and neck and do not impede the movement. The topline of the neck should arch and lengthen and not become 'compressed' and tight, which causes the back to become hollow. The focus of the rider in this early training should be on:

Restriction of the head and neck is the enemy of forward movement

- balance, breathing and lightness of communications together with building up the horse's trust and security (Figure 9.3).
- encouragement together with discipline.

A trusting horse will submit more effectively to a contact whereas an anxious horse's natural fear instinct will cause stiffness and tension, the enemy of harmony in training. A more relaxed and attentive horse should feel willing to cooperate with a contact from a 'listening' hand (Figure 9.4). It will be impossible to achieve correct contact without sufficient energy.

9.3 The horse is rebalanced and shows engagement and more self-carriage

9.4 Delfin demonstrates an energetic trot. The contact is containing, not restricting, the flow of energy

Contact is a way of containing the energy given by the horse into the 'sensitive' hands of the rider. If there is no energy or desire to move forwards, there will be nothing to contain, only an artificial flexion of the neck.

Contact comes from the willing mind of the horse creating focused energy in movement, and then allowing this to be directed by the rider.

If the horse is a little lazy, encourage him to work with vitality and become responsive to your aids for forward movement. So many riders focus on 'contact', using their hands to pull a horse into an outline but a horse can never progress in training without *energy*; something I *constantly* have to repeat when teaching.

Many problems with head and neck carriage stem from a lack of engagement of the hind limbs, which prevents a horse from working with sufficient energy to propel his weight forward, thus making it difficult to maintain balance and cadence. When the powerful hindquarters create a flow of energy throughout the spine the horse can then become efficient in his movement.

If a horse is mentally content and he has a bond of trust with his rider, he will be less likely to resist and the journey towards further submission and harmony can then progress.

Many problems in head and neck carriage stem from a lack of engagement

Sometimes draw reins and other gadgets are used to connect with the horse's mouth and a horse cannot physically resist them unless he rears or backs away from the forward movement. These methods rarely provide long-term solutions and can become the enemy of empathy and mind-to-mind communication. Side reins are effective when a horse is worked on the lunge but in ridden work they should never be used to force a horse into a fixed position.

A horse may lose the desire to work forwards if held in a fixed, uncomfortable position. How many human athletes are restricted by someone tying down and compressing their head and neck? Movement is important and horses must be *allowed* to move.

Gadgets are the enemy of empathetic communication

If each movement made by the horse impacts directly on the movement of his head, there can be no true relaxation through the spine, neck and poll. This type of restriction will prevent the horse physically and mentally from producing any work of value and destroy the opportunity for harmony; any movement there is will lose its regular relaxed rhythm. Anyone can intimidate and suppress a child or an animal with their training, but what is gained, a broken spirit perhaps? It takes two independent spirits, coming together as one, to dance. A trainer or rider must, like a male dancer, lead, guide and direct his partner with tact, feel and empathy.

SCHWUNG

The forward movement of the horse through an 'elastic' swinging back, created from energy and impulsion form the hind limbs.

Schwung describes not only an impression of the physical ability of the horse but also a mental attitude. Essentially, a horse is showing his joy in movement and it should be manifested in activity and elevation; he is glad to be alive, to be ridden and to channel his nature and vitality into his work (Figure 9.5). To produce gaits with schwung, the horse must feel disciplined but still have the ability to express his pleasure when working with his rider.

Stallions have taught me that they enjoy frequent exercise and appear most content, happy and relaxed after a work session. Their natural exuberance should be encouraged during training because it allows them to be true to their nature.

Several minutes in canter work can help to energize a horse and promote his enthusiasm. During the canter, a horse should step well under his body with the inside hind leg, which causes his carriage to be more elevated As the horse becomes stronger and more supple, his gaits will demonstrate more elasticity and expression

With experience, you can create a desire in the horse to work with the impulsion you need. The line between adequate and excessive energy is very fine and only with patience will the horse learn to understand what we require from him.

9.5 This horse is demonstrating true 'schwung' in his gait

Horses with a naturally large 'floating' or 'hovering' trot may not actually be working with sufficient energy and when asked for more impulsion they will sometimes lose their natural flow.

A horse needs to understand the meaning of 'energy from the hindquarters' and have his gaits guided towards further collection, lightness and balance. A degree of collection will be necessary before the strides can be lengthened. Extension is borne of the power created directly from the hindquarters (Figure 9.6). If the focus is only on lengthening the stride, before the horse understands engagement, the movement may be pushed further on to the forehand. Consequently the horse will be working out of balance.

If a horse is content in his work then he will have the ability to produce schwung, not through a forced position but through movement, straight from the heart.

> Horses with a large hovering trot may not be truly working with sufficient energy

9.6 Extension is borne of power and engagement from the hindquarters

STRAIGHTNESS

It is important to teach a horse to become straight in his movements from the beginning of his basic work. A horse, like a human is, by nature, often a little crooked or stiffer on one side than the other, which may at first make it difficult for him to move in a straight line. Tight and stiff muscles have to be slowly released and stretched to help the horse move straight. This will in turn increase his ability to move in any direction, without loss of coordination and balance.

Humans and horses can favour one side over the other

These traits will show in a horse's training. He may be quite stiff on the one rein, which will directly affect the way we give our aids. Steady lateral and circle work will help to generate more elasticity. In addition, a horse may have learnt a command on one rein but appear to be slow to understand the same command on the other rein; a rein on which he might also lack coordination and mobility of movement. A rider who is right-handed may well be using the right hand more strongly than the left without even realizing it. These are problems a rider needs to consider when giving commands on different reins. The suppling and strengthening exercises used in the warm-up session will help to give a horse more physical capability to move straight.

The collected work and advanced movements cannot be executed correctly if the horse is not straight because the extra weight cannot be taken by the haunches if the spine is not straight. Passage and piaffe require much impulsion and collection which cannot be achieved without true straightness. In order to assist this straightness, a rider's weight must be equally distributed and balanced between the horse's right and left side. Focusing on breathing will assist the rider with this 'centring' both physically and mentally.

A horse must first be straightened and then collected

COLLECTION

True balance in collection is the correct preparation for more advanced work.

In order to achieve balance and collection, each horse must be worked at his own pace for the sake of his physical and mental development. A horse may be powerful and strong naturally but if his training is rushed towards more advanced work he can lose confidence and pleasure in his work.

I believe collection is not just a way of going but is also rooted in a horse's emotions. For example, when stallions at liberty in a field perform classical movements such as pirouette, piaffe or passage, they are expressing excitement, pride and the sheer joy of movement in a light and energetic way. Delfin produces his most beautiful passage when he is allowed to express his pride and show-off a little. If I did not encourage this natural energy and emotion within him, the passage would not be a natural movement, just a mechanical one. As a trainer's abilities expand, he can learn to nurture and bring out these emotions and this way of going in the dressage movements and allow the horse to show his mastery of them (Figure 9.7).

For a horse, collection is not just a way of going but also an emotional expression of lightness and pride

9.7 The art is to allow the classical movement to become an expression of pride and joy

It is easy to recognize that all the scales of training are interlinked; each of them is needed to support the other. One training session may produce more cadence in the work, another more straightness. If a trainer feels that the horse is not working with sufficient straightness he can concentrate on specific exercises to correct this. For instance, straightness can be improved if a horse is not allowed to rely on the security of the sides of the school; he should be ridden straight down the school on either a 15 m line or the centre line.

The progression of work within this book helps to build more of an understanding of not only these goals, but also the ways to work with the horse in order to achieve these objectives harmoniously.

The following case studies relate to horses and people I have trained. They show how my techniques have proved helpful, giving attention to both the mind and physical abilities of horse and rider. All the names in the studies have been altered.

Case Study: Bob — 16.1 hh, 5-year-old Bay Thoroughbred-cross Gelding

Bob is a sensitive, yet promising horse but he is still young and insecure and relies on his rider for confidence. Lucy has owned Bob for six months and is keen to compete in the dressage arena; she is also interested in jumping and eventing but has wisely chosen to improve his flat work first.

Bob shows much potential in his aptitude for work and his basic gaits. He is sometimes highly strung and reactive and can get quite upset if he is not confident in his training. He is a horse who gives of his best but if too much is asked of him too quickly, he can become very agitated. Lucy and I discussed his feed, daily routine and regular dental care to ensure there were no potential problems resulting from incorrect diet, management or dental problems.

In his loose work, Bob moves energetically and freely forward and enjoys loose jumping. In his early training he was worked on the lunge for several weeks before being ridden and I have advised Lucy to begin her daily training with a few minutes of lungeing, whenever possible. Lungeing gives this highly energetic horse an opportunity to release some high spirits before settling down to working in a correct way on the lunge. This gives Lucy an opportunity to observe both his mood and gaits and will help avoid confrontation once she is in the saddle.

Lucy was focused on competitive work and felt exasperated when Bob offered resistance. She felt that his work could be so good but it was not consistent. He lacked the concentration that Lucy demanded and thus made them both become tense. Her goals for the future are well within reach, however, as Bob will eventually become a serious competitive prospect if he is allowed enough time to gain confidence in his ability.

Because Bob has such a great deal of potential, every time he shows an unwillingness to comply with Lucy's requests, she feels frustrated and does not realize that he is picking up these negative signals.

On one occasion I watched Lucy riding Bob in the school. For some minutes everything looked very positive with Bob showing relaxed and rhythmic gaits and rider and horse communicating as a team. Then Bob became evasive; he may have seen a movement or heard a noise that distracted him and, rather like a child, he was then unable to concentrate for any length of time. Lucy demonstrated her frustration by tightening her body and clamping her thighs against Bob's sides. His reaction was to mirror her tension which triggered an unproductive chain of events that needed to be understood and re-evaluated. Only Lucy could instigate this change by showing more empathy with his mood and directing him with calmness and discipline.

Lucy could use her power of reason to plan ahead but the horse would only respond through his natural instinct which depends on his current state of mind. If he is feeling happy in his work then the work can progress, but if fear and a lack of communication cause stress, the results will be manifested in tension and resistance.

When Bob put his head in the air, mentally he was somewhere else and when he felt Lucy respond with tension, this created more anxiety because he had lost the place of calm and discipline to where he could safely return.

I decided to lunge Bob with Lucy in the saddle so that I could take the responsibility for Bob thus taking the pressure away from Lucy. She then had the freedom to concentrate on her own responses. The build up of tension in Lucy's body had restricted her ability to move freely with Bob and she had lost her strong core of abdominal energy through the tightness in her back, shoulders and legs.

Lucy spent a few minutes focusing on her abdominal breathing, rebuilding a strong centre to help her support her natural self-carriage. I then asked Lucy to totally relax, almost slump, in the saddle. I did not want her to sit heavily in the saddle but just to concentrate on her breathing together with relaxation. Through this 'incorrect and slackened' position Lucy could begin to re-create her correct core stability and poise, more naturally. She could release the tension in her legs again, which allowed her to ride with her legs feeling lengthened and more supple. Energy was now being unlocked and her body began to move with more fluidity. Lucy became aware of how her stress had restricted the ability of her body to move in harmony with her horse.

We decided that when Bob became evasive and tense, Lucy should make a conscious effort to visualize relaxation and feel calmer about his behaviour, even humming a tune to herself and Bob (Figure 9.8). Basically, when she hears these alarm bells in her mind, Lucy needs to focus on changing her thought patterns to maintain harmony, both in her mind and with the horse.

After our training session Lucy began to realize how tense she had become about achieving instant results; she was putting pressure on herself to produce perfection. Any work that was not correct brought about her frustration which Bob immediately picked up. Lucy began to understand how her mind had affected her empathy in her riding. With a more patient and happy mentality both the horse and rider could settle down. If Bob felt distracted, his head would still come up but because Lucy let him understand that he could come back to his relaxed outline with no further anxiety, he returned to work more quickly, based on a better foundation of trust.

9.8 The rider can make a conscious effort to visualize relaxation and calmness

I advised Lucy to take more of a contact with the inside rein if she felt Bob was inattentive. If she rode with more flexion, with the horse working around her inside leg and hand, it was more difficult for Bob to become evasive and raise his head. Lucy was told to keep her inside hand low with the wrist turned in towards her stomach and waist, which would help her ask for his attention with authority. Once she received his attention and he began to work in a correct outline, she could relax the contact with the inside rein by releasing her fingers.

The expression 'to ask with authority' does not mean a rider should be rough or strong but clear and effective. A horse can understand a defined communication but will not respond correctly to many insignificant gestures. The obvious example is the rider who constantly uses his legs, jabbing into the side of the horse with every stride; the horse becomes immune to this constant nagging and will stop listening.

With experience we can all learn to be distinct with our aids so that a horse understands more clearly. When he responds, the release of the aids is his reward.

I continued the lesson with Lucy by asking her to circle and make sure that Bob was moving away from her inside leg and taking a correct flexion on the circle. She quietly turned her shoulders inwards slightly thus releasing her inside thigh. Bob felt the release and, with direction from her inside hand and leg, he began to move into a more consistent contact. He was then in a better position for Lucy to contain his movement with her outside rein and leg.

Walking on a circle, Lucy next asked for shoulder-in. When this was established she exhaled deeply and Bob moved into trot. Her allowing hand together with the shoulder-in had enabled Bob to work through his back, well positioned and in a relaxed way. The gait was loose, with energy from the hindquarters lightening the shoulders. Lucy continued to work forwards in trot maintaining the lighter feel gained from the shoulder-in exercise. Bob was being very attentive to Lucy now and seemed less concerned about outside influences. Lucy was giving him concise directions in a calm manner and they were working in tune with each other. She then spent a few moments walking with the reins held at the buckle, so that both rider and horse could relax and reflect on what they had achieved together.

Case Study: Jake – 17 hh, 7-year-old Chestnut Hanoverian Gelding

Jake was already a successful dressage horse when he came to me, competing at novice and elementary level. He presented with good natural rhythm in his gaits and was being ridden in a good outline although he looked at times restricted in his head and neck carriage. He did not take the contact forward but was tightening and shortening in his neck, causing his back to tighten and hollow. He did however lack engagement and his gaits, although naturally ground covering, were at times unbalanced. He did not appear to have the suppleness and freedom in his gaits to enable him to achieve collection. When a horse takes only a restricted contact from the front, his true movement will be suppressed and he will lean on the rider's hands for support rather than seek his natural self-carriage. Jake needed to be taught to work correctly from his hindquarters, to help him to produce gaits with more lightness and elevation.

Jake's rider, Sue, and I began by talking through Jake's lifestyle at home, his reactions to competition and his health and fitness generally; he appeared very relaxed and content in his home environment. Sue had been working with Jake for over a year and felt progress had been made. She had brought him on slowly with a lot of patience and she admired his attitude to work. Jake appeared so willing to please, but Sue felt he had much more to offer.

I always like to watch from the ground a horse working at liberty because so much can be learnt by observing the horse as a free spirit! I worked Jake loose for a while to assess his natural talent and character. He was not by nature a forward-going horse although he had big natural gaits. He responded well to Sue, but I felt at heart he was a little lazy. We introduced a grid of low jumps which seemed to spark off his enthusiasm and we began to see more suspension in his movement This elevation may be achieved when a horse is naturally enthusiastic and can give a trainer an idea of his potential ability when he is encouraged to work in this way.

Although Jake was producing rhythm, there was much more untapped energy in this horse that he needed to utilize if he was to carry his rider in true self-carriage. Lazy horses with big gaits can look like they are moving correctly to an uneducated eye; frequently, however, they are not moving with sufficient energy to produce true schwung in their gaits.

I noticed that if Jake led with the outside leg in canter whilst at liberty, he preferred to come back down to trot rather than continue around a corner in counter-canter. This was a result of his unbalanced movement caused by his hindquarters not following through. I also observed that he did not always bring his inside hind under his body when cantering on the right rein. Sue had to understand this lack of engagement and mobility and through lateral work and in-hand work help Jake learn to operate in a more athletic manner.

The lack of mobility from the right hind limb would have a direct effect on Jake's relaxation and submission through his poll. This could manifest as resistance from the head and neck, when in fact the problem was his lack of mobility from behind. It is quite often the case that an unsteady or resistant head carriage is created as a result of the hind limbs lacking energy or strength and freedom of movement.

Positive energy encourages movement to flow

Jake had been leaning on his rider's hands and leaning inwards like a motorbike taking corners when ridden in counter-canter.

We wanted to help Jake to learn to move in a more athletic way so that he would be better balanced and prepared to do the more demanding collected and advanced work later on. At this stage, Sue needed to ride a schoolmaster to learn how a more advanced horse can move in lightness and self-carriage (Figure 9.9). She would then be better able to assist Jake in finding his own natural balance.

Initially Sue rode Delfin on the lunge for several sessions focusing on her breathing, core stability and relaxation. Once she felt more confident of her own balance I asked her to concentrate on Delfin. I had been controlling my stallion on the lunge line but now I asked Sue to apply the sensations she had experienced to riding him in a more positive way. Sue had gained a new confidence and feel for lightness from Delfin, who is an extremely perceptive teacher.

In the mean time we used the following training methods with Jake: loose work and jumping; lungeing and trotting poles; work in-hand to educate Jake to use more energy and gain greater suspension from his hind limbs. He also learnt to mobilize his shoulders on a small circle.

After further lessons, Sue felt ready to work Jake under saddle again.

9.9 A schoolmaster can assist a rider to acquire the feeling of how a horse works in balance, lightness and self-carriage

We began with warming-up exercises on a circle to establish a true connection with the outside rein and a relaxed flexion away from the inside leg of the rider. I then worked Jake in-hand on a small circle whilst Sue rode him so that she could feel the athletic swing of his quarters. I wanted her to feel the increased engagement of the hind limbs and the contained energy and suspension that he was capable of producing.

Sue then worked through

some lateral work in walk. The slower gait gave both Jake and Sue the opportunity to concentrate on the correct positioning for the exercises. She then progressed to riding transitions: walk to trot, walk to halt, halt to trot and variations of collection and lengthening within a gait. She felt a much more springy and balanced trot with a greater feeling of controlled energy and his stride was not pulling her forward out of her position of balance but was developing elevation in a better natural carriage.

It could be a while before Sue was ready to try the counter-canter but I felt more confident that with the basics better established, the canter work would naturally improve. If the horse is to become a true gymnast, then his work needs to be progressive and steady. He will only lose confidence if asked to produce more advanced work before he is ready.

Creating Harmony in Training

Ride from the heart; enjoy your horse

The ability to ride from the heart and to enjoy the horse and his personality is the essence of horsemanship. The horse has an amazing power to understand our emotions and can respond equally to either our joy or stress. To become self-aware and control our negative thought patterns will always help to increase confidence for both the rider and the horse. Training is not only about correct aids and position but very much about communicating with joy and feeling. The horse has the capacity to understand and acknowledge our encouragement and pleasure which will in turn produce gaits which are fluid with positive energetic strides. A horse who is both confident and calm, and who trusts his rider for direction and leadership will be our rewards in training.

Our power of thought can either become our greatest ally or our worst enemy.

Our power of thought can become our greatest ally or our worst enemy

Being aware of our state of mind and the immediate effect it can have on the horse is the key to greater understanding and the keystone of strong training foundations.

The art of horsemanship can be compared to weaving with golden thread. Every positive and happy memory for the horse is another golden thread in the tapestry. Gradually, with patience, dedication and love, the tapestry gains shape, the picture comes alive. Devoted hours are spent with neither pattern nor form, nothing visual, just thread upon thread, woven with love. A vision of beauty slowly takes shape. Art is created with love (Figure 9.10).

Patience weaves good memories — good memories gain confidence — confidence gains ability — ability gains contentment.

The greatest lesson to be learnt on the journey of horsemanship is to develop a capacity for patience, patience and more patience. This important factor not only applies with regard to your horse, but also to yourself. If you can begin to accept your limitations but also allow yourself to experience joy in your achievements, then your inner harmony will have a profound affect on your horse. With these concepts

9.10 Gradually, with patience, the picture comes alive; art is being created with love

9.11 Respect and friendship are the foundations of a calm relationship

in mind it is possible to teach horses with empathy and confidence, building a firm foundation based on friendship, respect and trust to take you forward into more advanced training (Figure 9.11)

Small steps lead to the bigger steps which take you on the journey of learning. The goal, or destination, may be to gain knowledge and advanced skills but the day-to-day experiences can give you the gift of understanding, empathy, patience, creativity and love.

The journey of learning can be the gift, but not necessarily the destination

Juan Matute with Mariscal showing pride and elegance in his work (photo: Rafael Lemos)

Chapter Ten

Exploring and Advancing

'The ability to turn mistakes into learning – this is a worthy gift'
Jenny Rolfe

Having established good training foundations, we can now look at further exercises and advanced techniques.

Life for all of us is a journey involving constant change and exploration; this is a fundamental rule of life. Riding is also about exploration, not only with more advanced exercises but also with more perceptive skills of communication.

Relationships with our families, friends and horses will never just stand still. We always have to adapt to change because this forms the cycle of life. Sometimes within a friendship there may be a feeling of closeness and affinity but this can, through unexpected circumstances, quite suddenly turn to tension and frustration with a host of unwanted emotions and feelings. If the friendship is valued, however, a place of mutual harmony, relaxation and contentment must be sought. This is also the basis for empathy with a horse. I have often been asked if breathing techniques can really be an effective way of communication with a horse and the answer is most definitely, yes. Every horse has the capacity to tune in to our breathing, some may be extremely observant and sensitive, and others may take their time.

Reiner Klimke, one of the world's finest horsemen, said that if a training session went well, it could lift his spirits for the rest of the day and that he felt that he could almost walk on air!

Klimke successfully combined competitive aspirations with a love for, and harmonious relationships with, his horses. He clearly understood how to do this very well because he produced so many successful partnerships. He would know how much the horse could absorb from his training, the significance of thoughtful timing and knowing when to say, 'well done, that is enough'.

It is the responsibility of all trainers and riders to try to understand their horses, ensuring that they are not continually pushed to their limits either mentally or physically. Training is a man-made goal and we want

Nurture a horse's natural pride

the horse to retain his natural pride and enthusiasm whilst he is working as our partner and friend. Ensuring that a horse remains our friend after years of training is perhaps the most important aim for all of us.

The school exercises will prove helpful in producing a strong partnership in which the horse acquires an understanding of the rider. Both will gain pleasure from the work and the joy when harmony is achieved. Below are some of the feelings and experiences to be built upon, throughout training.

Sensations for the Rider

- A feeling of the horse's controlled/contained energy plus good rhythm and steady strides.
- A feeling that the horse is centred under the rider: neither leaning heavily, or pulling, against the hand nor slow to move forward from the leg, but balanced in between.
- The hind limbs should be well under the rider and not trailing behind (Figure 10.1).

- The forehand should be elevated giving the sensation of energy rising up in front of the saddle, i.e. a feeling of riding uphill.
- To experience how the hands have to be used, to ask, receive and give, in order to position the horse correctly to work in self-carriage.
- Asking the horse for energy: the rider's balance and strong centre (breathing) together with the voice, seat and legs (and use of whip) can inspire this.

10.1 The hind limbs should be well under the rider and not trailing behind

Learning always demands a certain amount of concentration which can induce physical tension. Training horses demands both physical and mental skills, but the more we can learn to visualize and develop feel with our riding, the less physical strain there will be.

You will also be perpetually reviewing and re-establishing lessons, movements etc., particularly if a horse falls back into old habits. For example, if the gaits appear dull, inspire and refresh with energetic forward movement. On the other hand, a horse might try to forge ahead and rush, dictating the speed of the lesson and trying to pull at your arms. If this happens, regain control and come back to halt. Re-establish your leadership in walk and halt. Riding many transitions will remind the horse that he is expected to listen and respond to your requests. Ask him to react to your aids and work in accord with your thoughts rather than allowing him to dictate the proceedings.

If we can encourage the horse to become really responsive, we are maintaining our leadership. An intelligent horse will always seek to change this equation, so it is a constant and ongoing task for the rider to maintain calm but disciplined leadership.

Calm, disciplined leadership

School Exercises

The school exercises, based on well-formed circles, loops and serpentines will help the horse to become more supple, attentive and active, if ridden correctly (Figure 10.2).

If a horse is lazy inspire him; if a horse is high-spirited, calm him

The rider must work towards being able to place the horse in a balanced position, from which he can turn in either direction with ease. Through transitions, changes of direction and variants within a gait (not just working or collected) the horse will steadily improve his athletic capability as he has the ability to produce many different speeds. (We talk about collected, medium and extended gaits but there are several variants within these collective terms.) If, for example, you think a trot is submissive and cadenced but lacks 'sparkle' and engagement, you can rebalance yourself and the horse by taking a deep inward breath and come back to walk. Re-energize the walk – think of the gait as an active, four-beat march – and then ask for an immediate (as if it were electrically charged) response into a vigorous forward trot. Carry this vigour into the canter and develop impulsion, swing and vitality in the work.

If a horse is feeling lazy and lacking enthusiasm, we will need to inspire him with more energy. If he is high-spirited and lacks attention, he will need to be calmed him and asked to focus his mind.

Continuously working in trot, with no transitions or lateral exercises, rarely improves the quality of the

10.2 Work on the circle can encourage the horse to become more supple and attentive

gait. Improvement comes with well-executed transitions, rebalancing horse and rider and creating further engagement with energy. The canter can be used to improve and revitalize an uninspired trot.

When you ride the downward transition from trot into walk, ensure the feel of forward motion is maintained. Ride forwards into an active march; do not fall into an amble! The rhythm will change from the two-beat trot to a four-beat walk and although the footfall changes, the feeling of impulsion should not.

Once you feel the horse is working correctly towards the outside rein and leg, continue walking forwards on the circle.

Downward spiral in trot

This exercise develops both balance and collection by asking for more engagement of the hind limbs and is helpful for focusing a horse's concentration if he is being inattentive (Figure 10.3).

10.3 Spirals

- After the warm-up period, ride a working trot on a 20 m circle.
- Turn your shoulders inwards slightly positioning your upper body on the path of a slightly smaller circle.
- Contain the hindquarters of your horse with your outside leg and take a steady contact with the outside rein.
- Maintain the inside flexion with an allowing inside hand.
- The rider's seat and upper body following the path of the decreasing circle will direct the horse onto the smaller circle.

- Reduce the circle to 10 m if the horse's training is advanced enough and if he is sufficiently supple to cope with the small circle.
- You should feel the trot begin to steady, decreasing in length of stride but gaining elevation. Keep the gait energized and regular.
- Spiral out on to the larger circle again using the horse's engagement to improve the forward stride.

Figure of eight with leg-yielding between the two circles

This lesson was used by General Decarpentry. The figure-of-eight movement will prove beneficial to teach balance and flexion as you work from one rein to the other (Figure 10.4).

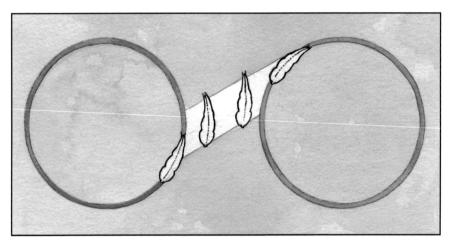

10.4 Figure of eight with leg-yielding between the circles

- Ride in working trot left on a 20 m circle.
- Before approaching the centre line, take a deep breath inwards to instigate a half-halt. Ensure the horse is well balanced between your hand and leg.
- The rider's hands position the forehand and shoulders to move to the right, which will lead the movement, and absorb the flow of energy created within the movement. The left leg behind the girth directs the hindquarters to the right.
- Contain the speed of the movement between your left leg and right hand allowing the flexion to the left.
- Continue the leg-yield for a few strides maintaining the left flexion.

- Position your right shoulder slightly back in preparation for the new circle.
- Straighten then reposition the horse for the new circle on the right rein. Direct the horse on to the new circle, which will change the inside flexion and the horse will move away from the new inside leg and hand.
- Circle right, asking for the new bend from your inside (right) leg into the left rein.
- Control the hindquarters on the new circle with your new outside (left) leg.
- Work on the new 20 m circle on the right rein and repeat this exercise on returning to the centre of the school.

Transitions

Transitions are the key to developing attention, submission and impulsion and should be introduced frequently at all levels of work.

In an upward transition, from walk to trot, for example, the rider must

10.5 In this upward transition, the rider is beautifully balanced with allowing hands and fingers

10.6 The lack of energy and submission is apparent in this downward transition; a deep inward breath will help the rider to achieve core stability to rebalance

'allow' the transition with the hands and fingers. The horse will resist if the rider asks for an upward transition but fails to allow the horse to work forwards into it (Figure 10.5).

In a downward transition, the rider thinks about rebalancing and breathing, making the half-halt, to ask the horse to steady and change his gait. The stronger inward breath, which supports the rider's back, may be necessary together with the rider closing the contact with the legs and fingers (Figure 10.6). Immediately the horse responds, the rider lets him walk energetically forward using an allowing seat and hand.

HOW TRANSITIONS CAN HELP

- Transitions procure the horse's attention and a prompt response to the aids.
- They provide opportunities for rebalancing and refocusing.
- Transitions are the key to producing more engagement.
- Resistance can be addressed with the use of transitions.
- A downward transition to walk provides a pause for correction if a horse is not moving straight.
- Transitions from one gait to another or within a gait (e.g. from collected to medium trot) can be used.

Gradually the transitions will supple and strengthen the muscles of the horse. In basic training the horse will begin to respond to the subtle aids of the rider and, over time, will develop a rapport with him, thus being better prepared for the more advanced exercises.

The half-pass
PREPARATION FOR THE HALF-PASS

In the previous chapters we have looked at various exercises including the shoulder-in and travers. The half-pass is a combination of these movements travelling across a diagonal line.

If you are not familiar with riding a half-pass, it can help to practise the movement without the horse. Walk on foot across the school on a diagonal line. When walking to the left, move your right leg in front of and across your body. Feel the weight transferring from one leg to the other. Place your fingers lightly on your hips and notice the swing and elevation required to allow your legs to move both forward and sideways.

When ridden, the movement, if accurately thought through, can be produced by using your shoulders, balance and breathing, with minimal leg aids. If you can prime your mind by recalling the feel of the movement from the ground, you will be well prepared to guide the horse through the movement. The horse does not understand 'half-pass' or 'pirouette' but he does understand a rider sitting up lightly and altering his balance with his shoulders to indicate the direction in which the horse should travel. He can feel when a rider has an allowing seat that does not block his sideways movement.

RIDING HALF-PASS

A few minutes of walking the horse in shoulder-in and travers will help to prepare both horse and rider for the half-pass.

Ride on the right rein in an energetic walk with cadence, maintaining a good rhythm. The horse should be alert, attentive and in tune with your instructions. Continue riding up the long side of the school in walk.

Ride a few steps of shoulder-in and then straighten the horse on the track; when approaching the corner of the school, ride a few steps of travers. Proceed to ride a 10 m circle ensuring that the control gained from the travers exercise is maintained throughout the circle. When you arrive back at the track having completed the circle, ride another half circle up to the centre line and prepare to ride the half-pass right from the centre line (Figure 10.7). Do not take too sharp an angle at first but prepare to ride the longer diagonal across the school. Take a deep breath inwards to rebalance and turn slightly towards the direction of the half-pass. The inward breath, together with your outside hand will gain control of the horse's shoulders.

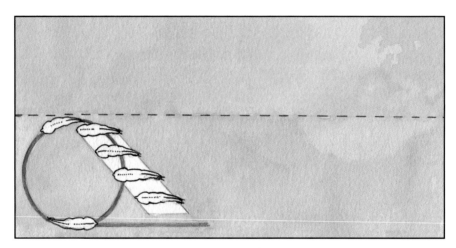

10.7 Half circle to centre line into half-pass right

The rider's hands again position the forehand and shoulders, which will lead him into the movement (Figure 10.8). Your inside hand should position the horse and then relax the contact when he is in the correct flexion (Figure 10.9).

If necessary, too much sideways movement can be restrained by your inside leg and the outside rein helps to control the speed. If the forward stride becomes lost and the walk has too much sideways movement, turn both your shoulders and the upper body to the front and ask the horse for one or two energetic forward strides before recommencing the half-pass.

If, on the contrary, the horse begins to work with too little sideways movement and too much forward movement leaving the quarters trailing, take a sharp deeper inward breath, rebalance and control the positioning of his shoulders. Then tap with your left leg slightly behind the girth and give a touch of the whip to bring the hindquarters back into the lateral movement.

10.8 The shoulders will lead the horse into the half-pass to the right

10.9 When the horse is in the correct flexion the rider can relax the contact and focus on balance and breathing within the movement

The head, neck and shoulders of the horse should arrive at the track slightly in advance of the quarters. As you approach the track, straighten the horse and guide the hindquarters across until they are correctly positioned to ride forwards up the long side.

With all new exercises you have to develop a feel for what is correct and this takes time and patience. Be prepared to give yourself time to learn new sensations in training, without creating excess tension.

Ride the movement with a soft and relaxed contact from the inside leg and hand, into which the horse can 'melt'. If we 'pull' him around with our inside hand, his head will tilt and it will cause tension. This will destroy the purpose of the exercise, which is to encourage suppleness, engagement and coordination.

I also use another half-pass exercise. Ride into the corner of the school and as you turn up the long side, prepare and ride half-pass across to the centre line. When you arrive, ride straight along the centre line to refresh the gait.

A horse should always be in the centre of your seat and motion. If you have to use too much physical pressure to bring the quarters across, this may displace your natural balance which will disturb the value of the exercise.

If there are problems in the half-pass, straighten the horse and continue riding across the diagonal in the intended direction. Reward his efforts with enthusiastic praise and a stroke of the neck, and let him walk on a loose rein whilst you re-evaluate the lesson; try to work out why the mistakes are occurring and what the solution might be.

Breathe —
give
yourself
time to
release
tension

Give yourself time to relax mentally, releasing any tension brought about by concentration. Remember to give a deep sigh at the end of a lesson. The horse will mirror your relaxed state and be more at ease during the next work session.

IMPORTANT POINTS REGARDING THE HALF-PASS

* Half-pass aids the development of lightness and collection.
* Preparation is the key to the movement.
* Position the shoulders and support with the outside rein.
* Contain the quarters with the outside leg placed slightly behind the girth.
* Do not aim for too sharp a diagonal until the horse is further advanced in his work.
* Aim for an energetic, but rhythmic stride.
* Ride each stride individually; do not allow your focus to drift several strides ahead along the diagonal line.
* Your breathing, allowing seat and energy from your strong centre should encourage each stride to flow.
* Ride the movement around the inside leg with a soft inside rein when correctly positioned.
* If the movement is not successful, straighten the horse and walk forwards across the diagonal.
* Enjoy the movement; marry your thoughts with those of the horse.

The half-pirouette (demi-pirouette)
RIDER PREPARATION

If you have not ridden a half-pirouette at walk, practise the movement on foot, as with the half-pass. Walk slowly across a diagonal with your shoulders facing the direction of travel and with your fingers on your hips. Feel the movement and swing your pelvis whilst moving straight. Imagine your two legs are the hind limbs of a horse and slowly turn in a half circle left, placing the right foot over and in front of the left as you turn. Feel the motion and rhythm of your hips swinging around on the circle. This is the type of allowing movement from your seat when the horse performs the pirouette. Practise this several times making sure that your upper body and shoulders are positioned to direct the horse around the circle.

HALF–PIROUETTE AT WALK

The half-pirouette turns through 180 degrees (a half-circle); the movement pivots around the inside hind leg and is performed with the smallest possible steps. The horse's shoulders move across, inscribing a larger circle around the hind limbs. It is important to maintain active, but steady, forward movement within the exercise. In more advanced training, the inside hind inscribes the smallest of circles, almost on the spot. In these earlier stages of training the outside hind inscribes a circle around the inside hind limb, which maintains a small circle forwards and across. The circle will become smaller as training, balance and coordination progress. The shoulders continue to take the larger circle around the hind limbs.

The half-pirouette at walk (Figures 10.10a–c) is an exercise that requires thoughtful preparation and a sense of rhythm and feel within the exercise itself. Working on the left rein, walk the horse around the school concentrating on straightness, cadence and energy. Proceed to work through the exercises of shoulder-in and travers.

When you feel that the horse is really obedient and responsive within these movements, ride around the short side of the school and ride a few strides of travers through the second corner of the short side. As you come out of this corner, turn your shoulders and upper body to align with the diagonal line. This will prepare the horse for the change of direction.

a

10.10a–c Half-pirouette at walk: a) the rider is pivoting her upper body into the movement, rebalancing with a deep inward breath; b) the horse is being asked to step forwards and around the inside hind limb; c) the rider is controlling the shoulders and focusing on her balance and breathing

b

c

Walk energetically but steadily along the diagonal line. Keep the horse straight, maintaining the control of the quarters established in travers. The hindquarters are then well positioned to execute the half-pirouette. (Figure 10.11.)

10.11 Ride travers into the corner, turn to walk across the diagonal and maintain control of the quarters to help the position for executing the half-pirouette

Maintain control of the horse's shoulders with the outside rein and take a deep inward breath to rebalance the horse, and then position his shoulders by pivoting your upper body into the movement to turn onto the circle for the pirouette. Place your outside leg slightly behind the girth and concentrate on taking one step at a time ensuring that the horse's hind limbs move forwards then across. With each stride, concentrate on breathing and the feel of the movement with your seat.

Ensure the horse is relaxed and yielding into the movement. Support him with the inside leg and inside hand, asking with the closed hand and then relaxing the fingers to encourage the correct flexion. Always think about moving forwards actively but containing the energy and balance within each stride.

When you have ridden the half-pirouette, continue in walk returning on the diagonal to the outside track. If you or the horse has become tense through concentration, walk several strides on a long rein, breathe deeply and relax. Reward the horse.

IMPORTANT POINTS REGARDING THE HALF-PIROUETTE

- Ensure the hind limbs are engaged and the horse has a feeling of lightness before the exercise is commenced.
- Control the shoulders.
- Use the seat and your breathing (breathe in to prepare for the movement, breathe out to flow with the stride) and allow the seat to instigate the rhythm with each stride.
- Encourage the horse to step **forwards** and around the inside hind leg.
- Keep the stride active but steady.
- Allow the horse to flex and relax into the movement.

The Benefits of these Exercises

The use of all these exercises in walk, with energy and cadence, will be most beneficial for suppling a horse. The time riding at walk through shoulder-in to travers, then into half-pass and half-pirouettes is well spent. Ride the horse from one exercise into another, concentrating on his active forward movement, balance, engagement and gaining his full attention. Working in walk will give you and the horse time to think about the movements. This gait can also help you to work correctly within the exercises, which will enhance suppleness, activity and collection.

After several minutes of lateral work in walk, ride forward energetically in trot to refresh yourself and the horse after the intense concentration; the trot should feel more elastic, better balanced and have improved cadence.

All these exercises will help the horse to become more athletic as long as we try to maintain harmony and rhythm within the work.

It is important in a relationship with a horse, to continually seek the physical, mental and spiritual balance. Not only will the exercises strengthen the horse physically but also the bond between horse and rider will grow into a deeper friendship founded on working together, listening to each other and finding a common place of learning and harmony; all vital components in a quest for progress (Figure 10.12).

10.12 The benefits of these exercises will be a more supple and balanced horse who is more attentive; harmony will be the goal

Riders from the Royal School, Jerez (photo: Rafael Lemos)

Chapter Eleven

Dancing with your Horse – Harmony in Movement

*'In dance something from deep within comes alive – a connection
between a man and the spirit and soul of his partner.'*
Jenny Rolfe

The word 'dance' means a series of rhythmic steps which portray artistic movements usually performed to music.

There is a vocabulary within the field of dance where such words as: 'elevation' (the ability to jump high in the air); 'capriole' (a leap in classical dance); 'galop' (a traditional nineteenth-century couple dance); *'en haut'* (a position with arms raised above the head); and *'en l'air'* (a step lifted from the ground) are used. These may have a familiar ring to the classical rider.

I have spent some time looking through a set of notes, written specifically for anyone wishing to learn the skills of the dance floor. It has been both fascinating and exciting for me as there are just so many similarities between dancing and classical training. I read through a list of helpful hints for people wishing to take up dancing and have listed them below because all of the instructions seem very similar to the concepts of classical equestrian training.

* Come with the correct frame of mind.
* Concentrate and focus – try to develop a 'feel' for the movements.
* Practise regularly, forming good habits through your repetition.
* Try to continue regular training with an instructor, with whom you can empathize and communicate.
* Always spend time warming up to avoid any physical injury.
* If a movement is not synchronized, this may be due to incorrect balance in the body.
* Understand the basics before trying to progress.
* Do not constantly criticize your partner – have fun and enjoy the experience.

I continued searching through interesting articles relating to dance, until the teachings of one particular woman really caught my imagination. The

Dance comes from the soul

American dancer Martha Graham (1894–1991) was born in Pennsylvania and had an incredible dancing career spanning many years.

Martha believed that creative dance came from the soul, and movement was created by the tension of contracted muscle from the pelvis (Figure 11.1). This continued in a flow of energy released from the body as the body became more relaxed. She was teaching the art of controlled breathing into the pelvic floor.

Martha went on to explain how dance could be felt in the contraction and release from the intensified moments of exhalation and inhalation. The deep controlled breathing increased the emotional activity, which meant that this experience was about teaching the body and not just about learning with the mind.

The contraction originates in the dancer's pelvis and the energy release causes a flexion of the spine. It occurred to me that this is a similar mobility of the spine that happens when a rider exhales deeply and allows the release of the spine and the seat. This was a revelation to me

11.1 Creative dance comes from the soul

because I knew from my experience of riding and teaching that the spine responds to lateral breathing, but I had no idea that similar concepts were used in the techniques of dance. It was enlightening to realize that Martha's techniques were borne of similar ideas to my breathing techniques for the rider. Martha taught that form is derived from emotion and that movement will become an expression of feeling. If riders can convey these feelings to their horses then they will become as one with them, both emotionally and physically.

Martha sought to give visible substance to things which can be felt and she called this 'the ability to chart the graph of the heart'. Following similar principles we too can learn to ride from the heart. Her style of dance and choreography drew upon many creative sources as diverse as Native American dances to the teachings of the Bible.

Chart the graph of the heart

You may think that dance is about athletic ability or can only be mastered in youth. But have you ever watched a physically disabled rider guide a horse from one fluid movement to another? He might not have the capability to walk without pain or some form of assistance, or may have a disease or injury which prevents him from living a 'normal' life but, in spite of this, he masters the exceptional skills required for riding both in balance and harmony. The 'able-bodied' do not usually consider it possible for a person with 'disabilities' to master the art of horsemanship with such physical limitations but many such riders rise above all these preconceived ideas and do, in fact, overcome extreme physical and mental problems. This would suggest that when we are not physically disabled in any way, the limitations of our mind can hold us back.

We think that the young and the very fit will ride with grace and ease. It is, however, sometimes the enthusiasm, dedication, love and a will to succeed that dictate the outcome. Some riders may not be capable of balance, as the able-bodied recognize it, because of a lack of mobility or loss of sensation in part of the body or limbs but they are capable of providing the type of control that enables them to ride in harmony with a horse extremely effectively.

We have looked at the importance of learning to use all our senses and develop feel and concentration with joy in our hearts, that is, the balancing of body, mind and spirit. Try to imagine the sheer

Ride with dedication, enthusiasm and love

joy people who have difficulty walking must feel when they are able to sit on a horse and feel the freedom of movement. They must fly! Their spirits must soar! And so it would appear that a significant part of the 'oneness' required for riding to become art, most assuredly still comes from within; from the heart.

Have you ever taken dancing lessons? Imagine that you are attempting to glide gracefully across the floor with your partner, but your mind is still cluttered up with problems from work. Maybe you have forgotten to make that urgent phone call or you have left a mountain of paperwork still sitting, accusingly, on your desk. In these circumstances it will be difficult to create a place in your mind where harmony, movement and dance can happen at all, but if dance is to have passion and be creative, that place must be found. Music, fun and laughter can lift our spirits. True dance gives the impression of effortlessness and lightness with a blending of the minds and energy of two beings; one being guided and led by the other.

Natural posture and poise enables balanced movement; this in turn will enhance the flow of energy required for two living creatures to move in harmony (Figure 11.2).

The Spanish Riding School in Vienna allows around five years for the training of their stallions. Further time is required for the horse to consolidate his understanding before he performs in public in the school. Along this path, the horse learns to comply with his leader, rider and friend, and the rider learns not to ask the impossible or to put too much pressure on the horse but to create empathy, in which the movement of two becomes as one, art is formed and riding becomes dancing.

For spectators, such a partnership uplifts the spirit and takes them away from their mundane everyday thoughts. They become inspired by the nobility and power of the horse and his willingness to work with his rider.

Create empathy in which the movement of two becomes as one

When we visit an art gallery, we are often amazed by an artist's dedication to composition, the magic of colour in the painting and the message that, possibly, lies within it and, as with the inspiring equestrian partnership, this experience can transport us away from everyday responsibilities and cares.

A good painting is not the result of technical ability alone; the interpretation of the subject will also be based upon the unique inspiration and creativity of the individual artist. God has created us all with a wide variety of personal traits and gifts.

Similarly, when working with and training a horse, the route which enhances both the personality of

11.2 Natural posture and poise will enhance the flow of energy allowing two living creatures to move in harmony

11.3 Jenny riding Falcoa; a picture of harmony and lightness

horse and rider has to be found so that a picture is produced. This is not a lasting image, as in a photograph or on a canvas, but an ever-changing, living form of art, harmony and joy (Figure 11.3).

In life not much stands still, evolution is a continuous process but we need periods of stillness to enhance our wellbeing with a balance between our physical and spiritual growth. This will in time be reflected by the horses we train, as they will become the mirror of our knowledge, self control and love.

There can be no beauty without love

Mestre Nuno Oliveira's riding abilities truly came from the heart and were not based upon a repetition of only mechanical exercises. He had a great empathy with a horse's mind and physical capability and used to say that he wanted to make a horse look more beautiful and proud. It is irrefutable that there can be no beauty without love; to dance with a horse, therefore, we must be able to feel and allow emotion to flow.

Reflections on Feel and Connection

Before a rider can dance with an equine partner he needs to cultivate ideas in his mind which will instigate the feelings of empathy and joy required to form a connection with a horse.

Before moving on with more advanced work, it is important to recall and revise some fundamental techniques that can help you explore the feeling of oneness with a horse. (Figure 11.4.)

Feel

- Visualize joy, harmony and empathy.
- Focus on lateral breathing which helps develop self-carriage, balance and release of energy flow.
- Look through soft-focused eyes and tune into your sense of feel.
- Sit in your natural self-carriage, totally balanced, allowing your seat to 'melt' with the movement of the horse.
- When you feel you are in harmony with the movement of a horse, gradually take up the contact with the reins.
- Do not allow your focus to be drawn towards your hands. Instead, sit with natural poise and posture.
- The power of the horse underneath you should create the feeling of energy and elevation in front of you; the forehand should feel like it is moving uphill. Allow your waist and stomach to advance with the movement.
- Maintain core stability with correct breathing,

11.4 Roberto Novao dancing with his horse

allowing your hands to become receivers of the energy. Use your fingers lightly to communicate with the horse's mouth by caressing the reins gently, maintaining a 'conversation' with the horse. The thumbs maintain a constant connection with the reins; the fingers provide the finesse by asking, receiving and then giving.

Envisage any of the following images to help you to gain feel with your fingers.

- You are holding a young bird that wants to fly away; your fingers gently contain his flight without crushing the delicate feathers.
- Imagine playing a tune on a piano, stroking the keys lightly to create the melody.
- Think about the strings of a guitar; they only need to be touched gently to create music. Each note is formed from the strumming of a string, the releasing of which allows the string to reverberate with its own music; the release enhances the music.

Connection

In order to make a connection with a horse, there has to be a mutual exchange of communication. The rider requests a response from the horse, which might necessitate positive reinforcement. Remember, first he has to work energetically and then, through a rounding of his back, he will relax the neck with flexion at the poll, after which he can be helped to find his natural position within self-carriage. When he starts to move in a lighter, more submissive way, he can be rewarded with a lighter contact.

Guide the horse to self-carriage, and then reward him with a lighter contact

If a rider needs to rebalance a horse or develop more collection, his fingers may be tightened momentarily whilst the rider rebalances himself and the horse with the deep inward breath. This deep inhalation widens and elevates the upper torso of the rider; a change the horse can feel immediately. The horse is being asked to come back under his rider, so that, as the rider lightens and expands his ribcage, the horse can also rebalance his movement and outline. Once the horse has done this, the rider can relax the contact with the fingers and breathe in a gentle rhythm with the stride. The horse's hindquarters can then take more weight, which frees the forehand to become lighter and elevated.

It has been discussed that no athlete, whether equine or human, can move in a gymnastic way if he is restricted in his movement, particularly from the head and neck. Locomotion requires that the head is the first part of the anatomy from which all movement flows. To disturb this energy flow will result in restricted movement and this will put strain on the spine and surrounding muscles. If a rider wishes to create movement, he must allow the movement to flow.

A horse will quickly perceive how relaxed or stressed a person is and the lightness or strength of his aids; a horse's great sensitivity enables him to tune into mood, body language and voice tone and he will receive and transmit all a rider's feelings. Once you understand the power of your influence, you can readily communicate with a horse and he will become the mirror of your mind.

Advancing and Developing Canter Work

There are several exercises that can be used to aid both balance and collection in the canter.

Canter spirals

Begin by riding a 20 m circle on the left rein. Turn your shoulders slightly on to the line of a smaller circle and maintain a steady contact with the outside hand. Support the movement with the outside leg just behind the girth, to encourage the decreasing circle. Gradually make the circles spiral inwards with each stride feeling like a small jump. Feel the horse begin to take the weight back onto his hindquarters and lighten his shoulders and forehand. Decrease the circle to about 10 m, depending on the horse's stage of training. When you can feel the benefit of this exercise, i.e. the horse taking precise, elevated strides, ride the canter forwards again, and spiral back onto the larger circle. You can then extend the gait to refresh the strides by using the forward, lighter seat.

This exercise is beneficial if the horse is pulling as he will have to

Use small circles to balance and collect; lengthen the stride to refresh

concentrate and move in a more balanced way to sustain the circle. Spirals will also encourage engagement, collection and obedience.

Counter-canter

This exercise requires a feeling of balance from both horse and rider and should not be taught until the horse is capable of a good degree of collection. Balance is developed as training progresses and the canter work requires a good degree of self-carriage before the counter-canter should be attempted. Riding through a corner in counter-canter will disrupt the horse's balance unless he has learnt to carry his weight from the hindquarters and mobilize his forehand. Initially when teaching the counter-canter, only ride a few strides at a time. This exercise can put quite a strain on a horse because it upsets his normal balance when cantering around a corner.

VISUALIZATION AND PREPARATION

To collect the canter take a deep breath inwards to rebalance yourself and the horse and then close your fingers on the reins. As you feel the horse rebalance and steady his stride, use the outward breath to release the energy flow and allow the seat to relax and flow with the elevation of the stride. Allow the breathing to widen your upper torso so that you can absorb the 'jump' in the stride from your strong centre and through your upper body. Ride with an inner feeling of pride, which will encourage the horse to move with more power and freedom from the hindquarters. The change in balance will lower the hindquarters – which will feel as though the horse is 'sitting into the movement' – and consequently allow the horse to move with more lightness. When you feel the horse 'sitting' more, relax your fingers to allow the horse's head into a position of unrestricted balance. As a result, the horse's head and neck will be carried higher naturally and must be allowed to move in lightness. The lighter shoulders and forehand and allowing contact will give a lighter more elevated carriage of the neck and head. The rider must not restrict this natural carriage but enjoy the feel of the lowered hindquarters and elevated forehand moving with contained energy.

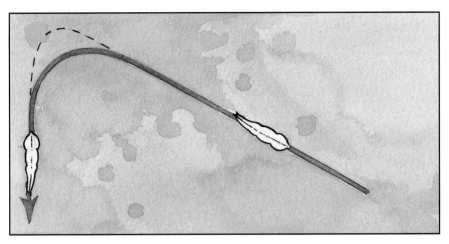

11.5 The correct track for counter-canter

When you can achieve the elevation in the canter and have a feeling of being as one with the horse, check that the energy level is correct by asking for extension. If the horse is leaning on your hands, use walk to canter transitions to ask for more obedience and submission. When the horse will collect and also maintain the impulsion for the lengthened stride, you have him well prepared for counter-canter.

Walk the horse on a loose rein in the direction of your proposed diagonal for counter-canter. Look for the track that allows plenty of time to begin the change of direction. Avoid riding too deeply into the corners but allow enough space for the counter-canter to avoid losing balance within the gait (Figure 11.5).

Maintain a feel of light, balanced energy

RIDING THE COUNTER-CANTER

Preparation
- Encourage a feel of lightness, balance, energy and collection within the canter.
- On a circle on the left rein, prepare with flexion to the inside and maintain lightness in the shoulder.
- Use 20 m circles to collect and lengthen the stride. Use a deep inward breath to rebalance and a deep outward breath to encourage energy and to lengthen the stride.
- From the circle on the left rein, ride down the long side of the school

in true canter. Ride away from the track in a shallow loop (allowing the horse's neck and head to follow the direction of the loop) maintaining the left lead and return to the track and ride forwards (Figure 11.6) The horse thus experiences a few strides of counter-canter and the rider a feel of rebalancing; the counter-canter tests the balance and straightness of the true canter.

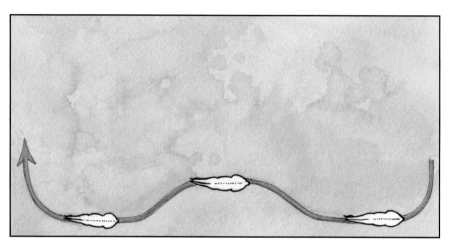

11.6 Ride a shallow loop away from the track

AN EXERCISE TO ESTABLISH COUNTER-CANTER

- When you have prepared for the movement by cantering with a collected and balanced stride, proceed in canter on the right rein. As you approach the short side of the school, make a 10 m half-circle to the centre line.
- As you reach the centre line, prepare to return on the diagonal to the long side. Take a deep inward breath to rebalance and look in the direction of the diagonal line. Ride straight down the line returning to the long side. Master each individual stride; do not focus your concentration across the school. As you return to the long side, prepare for a change of direction to the left.
- Ride forwards in the right lead towards the short side of the school, preparing well before the corner in counter-canter so that you do not make any sharp turns to upset the balance. (Figure 11.7.)
- Allow the horse to look in the direction of the movement (left) and help him to maintain balance by retaining a steady contact with the

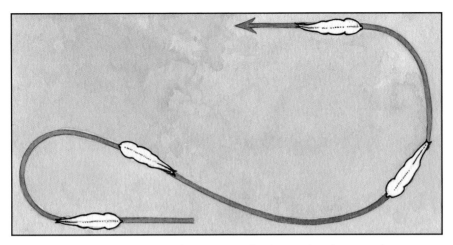

11.7 Ride a half-circle on the right rein onto the diagonal and into counter-canter

left hand. The left leg will help to direct the path of the quarters to support the counter-canter and the right leg will support the direction of the movement and maintain impulsion.

- Focus on your seat – your core stability – and breathing whilst allowing your shoulders, back and seat to absorb the movement.
- Turn your upper body into the direction of the bend; your right shoulder and seat bone will be positioned slightly forward (to align with the horse)
- Feel the movement of the hind limbs and the power as the horse steps under his body to carry the movement. The forehand will elevate and lighten. With sensitive hands, guide the horse in the direction of the movement.
- If you feel in good balance with sufficient energy, continue in counter-canter around the short end of the school.
  (Figures 11.8a and b.)
- Lengthen the stride riding straight up the long side then come back to walk.

A few good strides will help you to understand the change in balance more easily. You can bring the horse back to walk on the long side and ride on a loose rein as a reward.

Allow yourself time to evaluate how counter-canter feels. Did you feel balanced in the movement? Was there sufficient energy? Did you feel

11.8a and b Counter-canter: a) the forehand will elevate and lighten; b) ride in balance with sufficient energy

that the hind limbs were still underneath you or were they trailing? Did you allow the horse to look in the direction of the movement?

When the counter-canter becomes established, you are becoming well prepared to teach the flying changes.

Flying changes

If you have not experienced the flying change then it would be worth taking lessons on an experienced schoolmaster to acquire a feel for the movement before attempting to teach it to your own horse.

The more relaxed the rider can be when teaching this movement, the easier it will be for a horse to cooperate. He will probably find this new exercise quite exhilarating and exciting. Performed by a horse at liberty, this movement is normally used for rebalancing during a change of direction and will frequently be performed to express high spirits.

Imagine you are riding up a mountain taking the energy upwards with your movement. The position of the rider's shoulders is important so that the rider maintains a proud natural self-carriage. An deep inward breath causes a wide and full expansion of the chest, like a sail filling with wind, which creates more lift from the ribcage and allows the shoulders to release backwards and downward; this is the posture required to help the horse to execute the flying change (Figure 11.9).

We need to be ready to absorb the movement of the jump in the

11.9 Delfin showing good engagement in preparation for a flying change

elevated canter stride through our seat and upper body as the horse changes lead. Any obstruction from the rider will block the horse's movement, make him uncomfortable and he will not change with confidence.

It is particularly important when teaching the flying change that we wait for the horse to be in the right frame of mind. If the horse is too tense and excitable, performing these changes will only make him more so. The horse has to feel relaxed, confident yet energetic in his work.

Over a period of time the canter work will gain in rhythm, balance and collection as muscles achieve strength and suppleness and the horse gains confidence in his ability and balance, and the work must reach the following level of training before flying changes are introduced.

- The canter should be straight with good rhythm.
- There should be a good degree of collection.
- The horse should be both balanced and submissive when performing transitions from walk to canter and from canter to walk.
- Counter-canter should be established and balanced on both reins.

- The canter needs to be energetic, light and elevated on both reins.
- The horse should not only have the ability to steady the canter stride and 'sit' into it but also the ability to extend.

PREPARATION

Each horse is an individual and the more we understand the personality of a horse, the more easily we can teach the flying changes.

If a horse is extremely sensitive and responsive, he should be prepared with calm energy and repetition to help him gain confidence in his work. When the change has been ridden, he should be rewarded by being allowed to relax at walk on a loose rein.

A trainer's enthusiasm is excellent and can inspire a horse, but flying changes tend to create their own excitement and enthusiasm and so it may be more helpful to praise him with just a gentle tone of voice. After Delfin performed his first few tempi-changes, I made the mistake of being over enthusiastic with my praise. He was equally pleased with himself and threw in a succession of bucks! I had to calm both of us and settle for single flying changes for quite some time, until the memory of this exciting experience diminished.

On the other hand, a horse who is calm, cooperative and takes life in his stride might need a little encouraging enthusiasm before attempting the changes. If, for example, a horse can perform the collected canter, counter-canter and walk to canter transitions very effectively but is a little mechanical in his mind (i.e. he prefers steady repetition) I would then tend to take the canter forward and even ride over a grid of small gymnastic fences. This helps the horse to build his motivation and energy in a natural way, not from whip and spur, but by finding the work interesting and stimulating.

You can also ride the canter in a lighter forward seat which will help to promote more activity and roundness, with the weight of the rider distributed more lightly in the saddle.

GUIDELINES FOR FLYING CHANGES

- Ensure the horse is well prepared.
- Maintain straightness; it is important that the horse has the ability to bring his inside hind leg under him in balance. His back must be in

alignment. The outside rein maintains connection and the inside rein allows the movement.

- Ask for a shoulder-in 'feel': as you prepare for shoulder-in, invite the horse to bring his shoulders a fraction off the track; you do not need to ride the shoulder-in as a technical exercise but use this feeling of achieving lightness from the shoulders. Maintain lightness on the inside rein.

- Allow your inside leg and shoulder to come slightly forward to align with his inside leading leg and shoulder. Be prepared to alter this position with the new change of lead.

Lighten the shoulders

The flying change can be taught from various preparatory exercises.

FROM THE CIRCLE
Ride a 20 m circle in true canter and on arrival on the outside track, proceed in walk for only a few strides and then ride forward into counter-canter down the long side of the school for several strides. Walk before you arrive at the next corner. Practise this exercise, repeating the transitions at the same point in the school, until the horse is responsive and obedient to both the canter to walk and walk to counter-canter transitions. Then, instead of asking for walk, ask for the flying change at the same place in the school.

FROM THE HALF-PASS
The half-pass is another helpful exercise from which to prepare for the flying change. Begin by cantering up the centre line, with a good degree of collection, thus lightening the shoulders. After just a few strides, ride across the diagonal line in half-pass towards the track. As you approach the side of the school, straighten the horse and rebalance with a deep inward breath. Remember to sit centrally and use your breathing to maintain balance. Ensure that the hind limbs are correctly positioned centrally, absorbing the movement, to be able to execute the flying change. (Figure 11.10.) Take a deep inward breath (half-halt) and a steady contact with the outside hand. Rebalance, then re-energize with a deep outward breath, bringing your new inside thigh and shoulder forward and allow the elevation of the 'jump' through the

11.10 Ride half-pass from the centre line across the diagonal with a flying change as you reach the long side

upper body, as for the walk to canter transition. The new inside leg will be on the girth and the outside leg positioned slightly back.

FROM THE DIAGONAL

An exercise for the more laid-back horse is to place a low jump (about 45 cm [18 in] would be sufficient) about halfway across the diagonal line (Figure 11.11).

Prepare by riding a 20 m circle on the right rein, introducing canter to walk and walk to canter transitions and counter-canter. If the canter

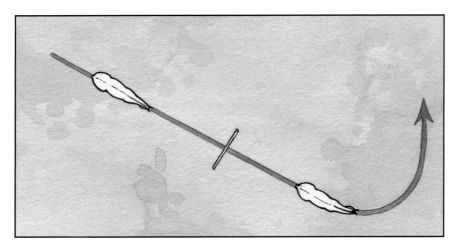

11.11 Flying changes on the diagonal using a low jump

becomes too strong, come back to walk. The principle of these transitions is to maintain the fine balance between energy and submission. These changes of gait will help the horse to gain the athletic ability required to master the flying changes. The number of canter strides will be dependent upon what you feel is necessary to improve and assist the balance of the horse.

When the horse is responsive and in a good degree of collection, continue on the right rein riding across the short side of the school. As you approach the corner take a deep inward breath to rebalance yourself and the horse. Ride around the corner and continue in right canter across the long diagonal. As you approach the jump, ensure that the horse is balanced using a deep inhalation to steady him if necessary. This deep inhalation will also help the position of your upper torso in preparation for the flying change.

Riding over the jump, allow your left thigh and shoulder to come forward, encouraging the new inside flexion. Your left leg will be on the girth with your right leg positioned just behind. This will encourage the horse to land correctly in the left canter lead. Ensure your left hand allows the strike-off into left canter. Maintain a good connection with the right rein. Proceed forwards in left canter, then extend the canter to refresh the gait, or come back to walk on a loose rein and praise your horse (Figure 11.12).

FROM A FIGURE OF EIGHT

The flying change can also be taught by riding two 20 m circles as a large figure of eight. Begin by asking for a 20 m canter circle left and on approaching the centre of the school, come back down to walk, before proceeding onto the new circle right striking off

11.12 Extend the canter to refresh the gait

on the opposite leg. Practise this several times and then prepare to make the flying change in the centre of the school. This method may prove more difficult as you are in the centre of the school with no outside wall to help you to focus when you begin the change of direction.

FROM CANTER LOOPS

You can use the long side of the school to ride shallow canter loops (5 m from the track). Prepare by riding a 20 m circle on the left rein asking for transitions from true canter to counter-canter (about every six strides). Proceed down the long side in counter-canter (right lead) riding a shallow loop away from the track. Make your 5 m loop and as you return to the track, ask for the flying change, and then proceed in true canter.

When a horse is learning flying changes, begin the exercise on his stiff side so that he can change back on to the rein he finds comfortable and on which he is more supple. This will make the changes more straightforward for the horse until the exercise is reinforced in his mind.

Once the flying change is consolidated, you can gradually work towards the tempi-changes, which will give you a real feeling of dancing with your horse.

TEMPI-CHANGES (MULTIPLE CHANGES)

Both horse and rider must be very confident with flying changes before the introduction of tempi-changes (Figure 11.13).

Tempi-changes can be taught initially on a straight line, either on the outside track or on the 5 m line. Begin by making a change then canter on with elevation and lightness in the shoulders. Maintain the collection, but if the stride is too short the horse will not find it easy to bring the hind leg through for a good uphill jump into the change of lead. The canter should be relaxed, light and energetic. If the stride feels too stilted, aim for exuberance within the gait before attempting the changes.

The horse will quickly learn to anticipate, and so it may prove

11.13 Janne Rumbough riding tempi-changes on Gaucho

helpful, initially, to teach tempi-changes in one place in the school; however, if you constantly teach the same number of changes in the same place, you may run into problems with anticipation and so it is advisable, once the tempi-changes have been learnt, to alter the routine. We have to try to use the memory of the horse for us and not against us!

We also have to recognize a horse's mood in order to prevent the exercise from provoking too much excitement. Some days it is good to work on the quality of the canter in true canter and counter-canter only; on another day single flying changes can be introduced, but the tempi-changes could be left for a while before they are reintroduced. If tempi-changes are continually practised in each training session, a horse will, again, start to anticipate and become overexcited, and the quality of the canter will disappear.

If we spend time developing a good quality stride, once the horse understands the aids for the changes he will be prepared mentally and physically to execute the exercise in good rhythm and balance.

After a short sequence of changes, ride forward to refresh the gait and if concentration has caused tension, come back to walk on a loose rein for a few strides.

Make a meaningful, heavy sigh and your horse will learn to emulate your relaxation by releasing a deep outward breath and then you can both relax for a few moments and enjoy the sense of achievement.

The timing of the aids

The art of timing requires feel and practice and it can be helpful just to watch a horse working in canter. Observe the sequence of the footfalls, visualize the motion for the rider and look for the moment to ask for a change of lead. This can become quite technical so try watching the horse through a soft focus and 'feel' the action. Observe the limbs and body movement and try to picture the timing of the aids from the ground. Further lessons on a schoolmaster will also help you to develop more feel and timing in your communication of the aids for the changes.

Use timing and feel for the changes

Piaffe and Passage

The good execution of these high-school movements is proof that true collection has been developed throughout training. For the spectator, the performance of piaffe and passage should leave no doubt that horse and rider are in total harmony and are simply dancing together (Figure 11.14).

Free in his natural environment, a stallion may piaffe or passage during times of extreme excitement. Our stallions will often perform piaffe just before they are covering mares.

We have already looked at some techniques for teaching the piaffe during the work in-hand and this is still the preferred classical training method for teaching a horse the principles of collection and ultimately the piaffe and passage. A horse requires sufficient suppleness, strength and flexibility to obtain the necessary collection to support these movements. A horse with an exuberant nature and powerful quarters who achieves engagement easily, might find the passage comes quite naturally. A more easy-going horse with weaker hindquarters will find it more difficult.

Passage and piaffe are movements that, with the correct preparation, should just flow. When the rider tries to emulate the movement with inadequate preparation or too much force, the essence of 'dance' may be lost. There is much power and elevation in the passage and the rider has to think more of absorbing the movement and allowing it to happen. The straightness of the horse is paramount as the spine needs to be correctly aligned for the horse to physically prepare for and

11.14 Rafael Soto performing the movement of piaffe

11.15 Classical *Mestre* Nuno Oliveira

execute these highly skilled movements of collection. A rider who has become proficient in the high-school movements, is well on the path to mastery of his own body as well as that of his horse. Balance, control of breathing and heightened awareness of feel will be essential for the rider at this level of work (Figure 11.15).

Piaffe and Pedro

I have tried to convey the importance of the relationship between horse and rider throughout the course of training. There are many excellent books of great technical merit which can help you with the training techniques for high-school movements. The purpose of this book is to create a greater awareness of the nature of horse and rider so that we can learn to work with the horse and not against him.

The following short story has a huge message; it says so much about the important bond between human and horse.

Ross Harper-Lewis worked for many years with Nuno Oliveira and was the manager of Oliveira's training centre near Mafra in Portugal. Ross has so many fascinating stories of the people who were drawn to the stables either as observers of the great *Mestre*, or attending for lessons.

One such lady – we will call her Iris – was well into her sixties. Iris proudly owned a charming stallion called Pedro; she wanted to learn more about the classical teachings and so Ross began to give her some lessons.

Ross was intrigued that a lady of her maturity would be so enthusiastic and totally committed to learning more about classical training. As Iris had expressed a desire to learn more about the movement of piaffe, Ross taught her the movement on several schoolmasters and was surprised at her sense of timing and feel. Iris was a skilled musician and Ross felt she displayed inherent ability and empathy which were obvious in her riding.

After several lessons, Iris admitted that she had taught Pedro to piaffe at home but she was unsure whether her aids were correct. Ross asked what aids she was giving the stallion to produce this movement and Iris replied, 'I just command Pedro to piaffe and he does!'

Ross was most amused and told Iris, 'This is great, you really don't need to know more than that. I wish I could do the same.'

This story contains so much wisdom and says so much about relationships and mutual understanding. Iris was totally unaware of her own gifts of communication, but Pedro understood.

Jenny with Delfin (photo: Barrie Rolfe)

Chapter Twelve

Delfin –
My Greatest Teacher

'Horses, a gift from God, mirror our personalities and become our best teachers.'
Jenny Rolfe

It is difficult to describe in words the huge personality of this Spanish Pure-bred stallion. Delfin arrived in my life several years ago and has totally changed my preconceived ideas and ways of thinking about training. My dressage training in the UK had taken me on a more technical path but I was to learn another dimension to training whilst communicating with Delfin. Our relationship was further developed in Portugal where I watched, and was taught by, classical *Mestres,* who rode from their souls and their hearts. These teachers motivated, inspired and influenced me to the degree that I was forced to re-evaluate all my previous beliefs and ideas.

Many of us will know wonderful horses during our lives but for a few of us there may be just that one special horse who becomes not only a wonderful companion, but also a 'soul friend'.

Delfin is my very special horse and he has revealed to me many aspects of the horse's mind. I have been taught by several great teachers, who have given me insights into many methods of training the horse but my greatest teacher has been Delfin. He has won the affection of everyone who has met him; they have come to respect and love his individuality, supreme intelligence and talent. Dressage movements with Delfin are full of life, fun and vitality and are most definitely not just functional or mechanical. The spirit of this wonderful fellow creature has created an indelible stamp upon his training, and also on me. Why has Delfin become such a great teacher? I have learnt with Delfin that nothing less than total self-awareness and focus of my mood, balance and breathing will gain a positive response. He always mirrors my frame of mind, and my every nuance of balance; he has the ability to reflect my personality and body language. He immediately senses tension, sadness and frustration. Equally he can exude energy and joy when he feels my pleasure and happiness.

Our greatest teacher is the horse

For us all, life is a journey that, as we travel along its path, can teach us the importance of loving, caring for and nurturing those around us. As we venture further along the path, we will learn more about our own personalities and this is where our horses can become such powerful teachers, as, like Delfin, they will in time mirror those personalities.

Meeting Delfin

After arranging a trip to Spain with a view to finding a suitable stallion, I arrived at the first stud farm on the agenda: the prestigious farm of Pedro Cardenas. This stud mostly sells its horses abroad, mainly to America and Mexico, and so my husband, Barrie, and I felt privileged to be allowed to visit it. On arrival at the stud, the large brand denoting the farm's aristo-cratic bloodlines loomed over us at the entrance. We walked through the corridors of the stables housing the most gracious stallions; each of them a magnificent representation of nobility and beauty. The foreman took Delfin into an arena (which resembled a sand pit on a steep slope) and I was told that Delfin XII had been Pedro Cardenas's bullfighting horse (Figure 12.1).

12.1 Pedro Cardenas on Delfin

We watched this beautiful silver-grey stallion in complete awe! He was the epitome of nobility, exuberance and power and, as would be expected from the Cardenas line, he was a horse of considerable beauty.

He was taken through his paces around the arena but, to my eye, he looked bunched up and tight; a not-surprising state considering the proceedings were being observed by a menacing black bull with ferocious-looking horns.

After several minutes I was asked if I would like to ride Delfin, so I walked with some hesitation into the ring with the bull still standing menacingly nearby. I mounted Delfin and he immediately responded to the lightest of aids, was totally attentive and wanted to please. He felt supple and athletic with the most amazing feel of quivering energy and his canter was powerful, yet light and uphill. I felt that I could sit there all day holding a cup of tea or, more appropriately perhaps, a glass of sherry! I was totally smitten.

After I had ridden Delfin we were taken around the stud to see the mares and foals in the fields. It all reminded me of the Piber stud in Austria, part of the Spanish Riding School, with its stunning white mares and gorgeous black foals. The Cardenas mares were outstanding and many studs would be proud to own mares of such quality, bone and substance. Sadly we had to say farewell to the Cardenas stud as I felt I needed to see and ride more horses; Delfin was the first I had ridden on this trip.

The following days were spent visiting several dressage yards and riding many other horses but I found them to be less flamboyant than the more gymnastic bullfighting horses; a fact that opened my eyes to the type of temperament I would be looking for in a horse.

The demands of the dressage arena are accuracy and concentration, from one marker to another within the structure of a known test. The bullfighter does not know what the bull will do and his horse has to be totally obedient to every subtle change and movement of the rider. The penalty for the lack of an immediate response is not a 0–3, but a painful meeting of the bull's horns and the horse's flanks.

The bullfighting movements of the *rejoneador's* (the mounted bullfighter's) skills (*rejoneo*), have been developed to create a beautiful dance full of emotion and energy. This artistic form of *rejoneo* may lack some technical merit by modern competitive dressage standards, but I have seen nothing that compares with its feeling of spirituality and oneness between man and horse.

I watched Jesus Pirez, a bullfighter, riding his palomino horse; the two appeared to fly and amazed all who watched them with their grace and fluency. This was the power of dance.

After having ridden several stallions I was beginning to realize that no other horse was quite like Delfin; the instant I had started to ride him, we had a rapport. It was an unforgettable meeting of minds. I had a feeling that my life was about to change for ever and this would also prove to be true for Delfin. He was coming home!

Early Days in England

When Delfin arrived in England (Figure 12.2), the early days presented us both with a steep learning curve. Delfin had been stabled for twenty-four hours every day, other than when he was being worked, for most of his life in Spain. He appeared very tense and unsettled, performing passage and piaffe in his stable. Slowly I tried to win his confidence by sitting outside his stable. I sat there often, peeling endless vegetables, reading books or anything else just to while away the time because I just wanted him to feel secure and calm in his mind. His inquisitive nature soon began to take over and he would come and peer over the stable door.

I put the radio on during the day, in an attempt to calm him and also began to introduce him to grass. Delfin did not understand freedom or space so it would have been unwise to just turn him out in the field. If a human has suffered imprisonment or a suppressed lifestyle for many years, there would be major problems to overcome before he could gain the confidence to deal with new situations. There

12.2 Delfin outside the house

is a strange type of security that can ensue from a restricted and confined environment.

Each day I would lead Delfin, in as quiet an environment as possible, into a field and just stand or sit with him. He would snatch violently at the grass, always more curious about his surroundings but it was quite a while before I could take off the rope and leave him alone in the field. When I walked to the gate he would follow me back and only return to his grazing if I stood to watch him. If he saw me make any attempt to move away, he would immediately gallop back towards the gate.

It took many weeks of time and patience, to slowly build up his confidence so that he would graze alone and even then I would have to work around the stables keeping him in my sight. Delfin would position himself in the field so that he could watch me or just stand and look across at what was going on.

His life in Spain had been very disciplined and restricted and so we also turned him loose in the school to let him play a little. When I began to loose school him I realized that he was mirroring all my movements: if I turned or moved he would do the same. He appeared to want to become an important part of my life.

Delfin was to become the teacher who would show me the importance of listening and tuning in to a horse, not in a logical or mechanical way but with feeling and emotion. A truly amazing and revealing empathy was to develop between us. We were becoming kindred spirits both trying to learn from one another. (Figure 12.3.)

Early Training

Our early training sessions taught me so much. Through his work in Spain Delfin had developed a way of going under saddle that would take years to change. He was very tense with highly charged, nervous reactions and his trot was bunched up, being almost executed on the

12.3 Delfin a week after he arrived in England

12.4 Delfin beginning to work forward and cover the ground in trot

spot, and it did not improve at first, even with walk and trot transitions. This highly charged tension controlled all his movements but he did seem to settle more in the canter. A mounted bullfighter works in canter for a great deal of the time and it appeared that trot work was a foreign language to Delfin. He had also been used to having commands in Spanish and so, to help him understand my requests initially, I used a few words in Spanish for basic instruction. We had also started to communicate in our own 'language'; a deeper understanding was developing.

Because Delfin did not understand trotting forward rather than on the spot, I had to find ways of teaching him what was required. Most days, after working him on the lunge, I would begin by riding in walk and then get him to take a few strides in trot before quickly moving into canter. We would stay in canter for a while before I asked for a downward transition into trot. The first few trot strides would take us forward, which was a huge improvement on the stilted trot he had been presenting before. I then came back down to walk and praised him, stroking his neck and allowing him to stretch his top line forwards and down. These exercises progressed slowly over the months until he learnt to take the trot movement forwards and relax more within the gait (Figure 12.4).

Early in his training I thought that trotting poles would be helpful to lengthen his trot but when he saw the poles his initial response was total panic; he looked upon them with the greatest suspicion but did change his mind over a period of time. Delfin now works loose over poles with no tack, responding only to my body language, voice and breathing. This type of trust has taken years to build up, with no quick fixes, just time and patience, and I believe there is no substitute for this if you want to build a harmonious relationship. Trust has to be our goal when working with horses.

The most testing lesson for me has been learning to maintain Delfin's trust and confidence. He would often try my patience and I felt that a strong tap with the whip would be in order to gain his attention. The problem was that after such a reprimand Delfin would become extremely agitated and the chance of any relaxed work would totally disappear. This is one of the reasons why Delfin has become my greatest teacher, whenever I thought that I had the answers, he would produce another aspect of behaviour for me to deal with. If I chose the route of patience and more patience we did reap rewards in our communication.

> The greatest lesson is to develop trust and confidence

We have to assess the reason for difficult behaviour and if the cause is anxiety or fear then using a whip will never produce a calmer horse. In these situations we have to become clever in our thinking in order to encourage the horse to be 'on our side'.

Frequently I changed exercises or re-evaluated my ideas to make it possible to bring about a more positive response from Delfin. For instance, he would always lose forward momentum when approaching a gate in the school. I assumed that he still thought that the gate would suddenly open and a bull would charge towards him. Some memories were well established in his thought process. When we had moved away from the gate he would try to rush forwards as if he were being chased.

Feeling very frustrated one day as I could not seem to find a solution to this problem, I decided to halt near the gate. Delfin's body was a quivering mass of energy and he felt as if he might be about to explode in any direction. I gave a deep sigh, probably as a result of being so frustrated by his refusal to listen to me. I walked him for a few more strides, came back to halt and exhaled deeply again. Immediately I felt tension flowing from Delfin; he seemed to be responding to my sighs. Perhaps all his excess energy was also proving too much for him. Horses have amazing memories and I believe that if they have suffered serious anxiety or abuse, they experience an 'action replay' in their minds, which brings all these things to the fore in a similar situation.

If you are talking to someone who suddenly yawns, it is extremely difficult to stifle a yawn of your own. This concept of copying behaviour, breathing and body language is, I believe, a characteristic of both humans and horses. If you spend some time observing horses in a field you will see that they copy each other, always observant of each other's body language and every movement. Sometimes they appear to move, and even chew, in unison! We are all affected by what we observe and can instinctively tune in to the breathing and body language of others. For instance, you may walk into a room and detect a feeling of stress between two people. It may not always be visually perceived, but it most certainly can be felt.

Once whilst watching Barrie walking up the field with a wheelbarrow; Delfin gave several high-pitched snorts and took flight in a state of heightening anxiety and fear. Neither of us understood what was happening to him. Several months later in Portugal we saw some bullfighting horses going through their initial training; a boy pushing a wheelbarrow with horns secured on the front was taking the place of the bull. He charged towards a horse and both horse and rider had to respond immediately to avoid the 'bull'.

We now believe Delfin may have gone through this type of training whilst in the bullfighting yard in Spain and he has never forgotten it, neither do I think he ever will.

Delfin had taught me another valuable lesson: when horses respond in a negative manner, you have to ask yourself why. If these intelligent, sensitive creatures with amazing memories are given the chance to express their emotions, they will be more willing to accept our instruction and discipline. If anger is expressed when a horse is emotional or fearful, his training will be suppressed. Communication demands patience, spiritual insight and a feeling for our own and the horse's emotions. This requires discipline of a trainer but the rewards are worth the commitment.

Progress

I worked with Delfin consistently for about a year along these lines, trying to establish a bond of trust between us. During the training I was steadily aiming for more relaxation and fluidity within the gaits whilst developing straightness and rhythm in his work. It was easier for Delfin to produce half-pass and lateral work, than for him to work forwards and cover the ground. I realized the more advanced movements could physically be quite easy for him but at that time we had to concentrate on our basic training. I was also keen to get him to focus on his work, a task which took both diplomacy and tact, trying to keep a calming cap on an erratic mind.

At times, progress seemed painfully slow. There would be a few settled sessions when Delfin paid attention and then for some reason he would show evasion and inattentive behaviour. If at this point I showed my frustration, the trust we had built up would have disappeared. I knew that I could have put pressure on him to comply with me, but somehow I felt that we would have lost sight of the joy and freedom of movement. He would produce only stilted gaits if he felt under too much pressure.

Once again, Delfin had become the teacher and I the pupil. A horse can be made to comply by the use of force, but the true principles of classical training will be fundamentally lost. This can be likened to a marriage where two people should be able to resolve their differences verbally but once a partner brings violence into the equation, all trust and respect disappears. For any relationship to become meaningful there has to be a reciprocal agreement to listen to the view of the other person. When anger and temper are resorted to, it is an admission that a better way cannot be found to get a point of view across.

If a communication breakdown happens it is time to take a step backwards and re-examine the current paths of communication if progress is to be made. For the classical horseman this means never acquiring submission by domination and fear. If a horse is intelligent, he will at times challenge his trainer and the challenge must be met with respect and discipline, the latter being given calmly and without anger, and with the expectation that a request will be carried out. A well-timed reprimand may be justified but should not be the first tool of communication. There may, however, be times when a horse demonstrates a lack of respect or exerts his dominance. We then need to reinforce our leadership tactfully, and with good timing, to re-establish his respect.

These early lessons with Delfin, carried out with thoughtful training and patience, were tough and sometimes I was left with a feeling of non-achievement. During the six years I have spent with him, however, I realized that when we appear to achieve nothing of consequence, we are achieving it all. Less may be more and sometimes calmness and quiet can be everything.

I have also learnt that it is possible to become very focused on the work of the day and lose sight of the bigger picture. The relationship is far more important than any single goal in training and sometimes we have to settle for less than we hope to achieve during a training session. If we have the courage and wisdom to accept something good, and be thankful, even when our expectations are not being fulfilled, we are learning the skills of the true horseman.

Working with the Classical Mestres in Lisbon

I have marveled at the empathy in horsemanship and oneness achieved by some of the leading bullfighters and classical trainers in Portugal and Spain. I had a strong conviction that I wanted to explore this classical training path with Delfin, so that we could further our relationship and education. With this in mind I traveled with Delfin to Lisbon, Portugal to the yard of Dr Guilherme Borba where I was to be taught by his nephew, Antonio, who is a Chief Instructor at the Portuguese School of Equestrian Art.

I spent much time there riding, observing and writing and have listed below some of the important lessons I learnt from observing Antonio working his horses.

- The importance of being completely focused on just yourself and the horse.
- The importance of balance.
- The development of timing, feeling and knowing when to reward.

- Learning to read the horse: anticipating his response.
- The importance of being a centred rider (core stability).
- The improvement of skills in the name of art.
- Confidence with empathy.
- The importance of accuracy in movements.
- Learning through repetition.

Focus only on you and your horse

I watched Antonio teach Delfin piaffe and passage. Delfin's exuberant nature made this a pleasure for horse, rider and spectator! Delfin was taught piaffe in hand and then progressed to the ridden exercises. (Figure 12.5.)

Trotting poles were used to encourage forward and deep work. Delfin needed this throughout his training because learning to improve the basic work will always be his path to advancement. I also placed the trotting poles closer together, to encourage more collection and elevation, in preparation for the passage.

Delfin will still come 'back towards me' when he becomes tense but he now understands that he must always have the desire to go forward in his work, even within a stressful situation. If a horse is taught to go forward at all times then it is unlikely that he will choose to nap or spin around as an evasion to instruction when under pressure. (Figure 12.6.)

I had hoped to establish the flying changes whilst in Lisbon but, although Delfin began to consolidate them there, they became more consistent on our return to England. The flying changes and the tempi-changes became a joy for us when working in our windswept arena on Exmoor!

12.5 I learnt much about focus and concentration by watching Antonio Borba riding Delfin

On Returning to England

Once we were back in England, I longed for the warm, balmy days of Portugal. It was so much harder to achieve the same harmony in the harsh climate of southwest England because Delfin loves the warmth of the sun and relaxes in the Iberian climate (Figure 12.7). I did, however, arrive home with transformed ideas about training horses and I have been slowly developing my methods, based on Antonio's teachings.

12.6 Jenny training in Lisbon with Antonio

As my thoughts on training continue to evolve I often recall the precious times in Portugal. I have many videos and books of notes taken daily during my training. It has been important for me to make notes after every training session for the last twenty-five years.

I have continued to progress with Delfin, just one step at a time, and he has begun to show a more willing and attentive attitude to his work. I have re-introduced the flying changes into his work, minus the enormous joyful bucks; he is now settled enough in his routine to contain his exuberant

12.7 Jenny and Delfin enjoy working in the Portuguese sunshine

behaviour and perform the changes more easily. We can ride tempi-changes every three strides but there are still the odd occasions when Delfin can no longer contain his *joie de vivre* and he performs his bucks once more.

I have to be cautious when praising Delfin. I become very enthusiastic when he works well, but I soon realized that when I am 'too joyful' Delfin will over-react and become too confident and overexuberant.

Working a stallion is a compromise between asking for his attention and obedience and allowing him to express his joy in his achievement. This harmony and balance is the essence of a successful relationship; a negotiation between rider and horse.

Refining our Communication

In an earlier chapter I explained how the breathing techniques were a significant breakthrough in our communication. Every horse will listen to the breathing methods that have evolved during my time training Delfin. The techniques are already proving an inspiration to many people who seek more subtle communication with horses.

The loose work is very important to Delfin. He observes and responds to my every movement, at liberty with no tack, just his free, but compliant, spirit. If he chooses to work with me so agreeably when he is free, he will take this positive attitude into the work under saddle. Sometimes, if lessons have been a little tough and Delfin has worked hard, a session of loose work consolidates our relationship without the tension of producing good quality gaits and accurate movements.

The Greatest Lessons

Sadly it is human nature to become desensitized to our own actions. I have worked with teenagers involved in serious crime and an act that starts as simply a cry for help or just fairly innocent behaviour can develop to give the perpetrator a sense of control and misguided achievement. The more people become accustomed to stealing and abusing others, the less they comprehend the misery and fear they leave behind. Many criminals would admit that they have little feeling for the people they have abused. The initial sensitivity is destroyed by repetition and the thirst for personal gain. There is currently a programme which introduces criminals to their victims thus forcing them to face the stress they have caused people; it is hoped that this strategy will help these criminals not to re-offend.

Maintain two-way communication, don't be a dictator

Maybe there are lessons here for riders and trainers. We need to listen to the horses in our care, ensuring that their behaviour never becomes a plea for our help and understanding. If we can undertake the responsibility of fairness and consideration we will be able to listen and respond, thereby maintaining the kind of communication that does not lead to dictatorship (Figures 12.8a and b).

The more time and patience spent on working towards a good relationship, and not trying to dominate it by becoming a dictator and bully, will ensure the long-term results of satisfaction and spiritual fulfillment for both horse and trainer. It might seem the easy option or a quick solution to beat a horse into our way of thinking, but we, like the habitual criminal, can end up becoming desensitized to our own actions. The response of the horse to continual harassment will in time make him become desensitized to the human. He may appear to cooperate but his soul and individual personality will become soured and his movements will become mechanical; his heart will not be in his work or the relationship.

You have to be disciplined enough to master your own personality otherwise you will not successfully master a horse. This is why the art of classical horsemanship takes a lifetime to achieve. The classical path is sound and all who follow this route can learn more of the fundamental qualities missing from today's way of life.

I once thought that teaching a horse was about learning and refining the tools of training. The lessons I have learnt since being part of Delfin's life, however, have a much more profound value. Delfin has taught me to

12.8a and b A dialogue about listening and responding

continually be prepared to learn more and to be open minded. I have also learnt that human nature is never 'all knowing' and we need to let go of our ego and allow the spirit of a horse to reach out and communicate with us.

True horsemanship demands time, patience and a, sometimes painful, honesty. As our horses start to mirror our traits, we may come face to face with the reflection of behaviour which shows that we might be lacking in kindness, confidence and a desire to please.

Lessons can be a brutal experience at times but, with honesty, we can develop a way forward based upon a clearer picture.

There is a saying that when we devote ourselves to God's creation, such as farming the land or caring for all creatures, then we are in turn brought nearer to our own Creator. Horses can offer healing, inspire wisdom and are capable of helping us to find a deeper understanding of the ways of nature and of God. We can all benefit so much from taking the time to 'just be',

Our horses reflect us and become our mirrors

with no ambitious agenda or driving force. Just to have the time to forget everything and concentrate solely on the beauty and nobility of the horse will provide us all with inspiration.

I feel privileged to be part of Delfin's life as he is truly my soul friend. Every loving relationship lasts forever, as I believe the spirit of love is immortal (Figure 12.9).

12.9 Delfin and Jenny enjoy harmony in work

'The Horse, Our friend and Teacher' (photo: Rafael Lemos)

Chapter Thirteen

The Horse, our
Friend and Teacher

'His back a throne of feathers...the chosen one of Kings.'
Juan Llamas

I felt inspired to write this book because of my love of horses and I hope that some of my methods and ideas will encourage a further understanding of the horse and his nature. Horses can prove to be a never-ending adventure and bring much joy and richness into our lives.

I have sometimes watched horses obviously unhappy in their work, with the rider seemingly totally oblivious to the horse's state of mind. I have been guilty of this myself and I will no doubt continue to make mistakes but the difference now is that I am much more aware of what my horse is thinking and how he is responding.

We tend to think of a situation as being right or wrong, correct or incorrect but the horse does not see his relationship with us in this light and I am extremely aware of this. It is the trainer's responsibility not to project human feelings and goals on to him but to try to work with him mentally, physically and spiritually.

Our quest for understanding should not be limited to perfecting movements in dressage but to gaining empathy with the horse and his understanding. In this way we can become both a friend and a teacher. The learning curve for me has been to seek the importance of true horsemanship.

Horses have the ability to bring a peace and calm to the moment (Figure 13.1). These moments can transport our thoughts away from the daily routine, enhancing a feeling of calmness and tranquility.

My horses always greet me and we stand together, human and horse, neither speaking the same language; through a mutual desire to communicate I think we have, however, found a common place. Our language is borne of an awareness of each other's mood and nature, together with mutual respect and love. Our journey is not over, there is so much more to learn. Respect came first, then a feeling of mutual trust.

13.1 There is a timeless peace being in the company of horses

From this grew a deep spiritual love which has given our relationships and training more meaning. Teaching horses requires concentration and discipline but with it can come relaxation, fun and harmony. All the varied emotions of man and horse can come together within the gaits and the framework of training. This gives training a deeper meaning which transcends the individual movements themselves.

I know there can never come a point when I can say that there is no more to learn, I understand it all. This is why there is no place for human ego with horses, only a place for quiet learning and a love of horses.

The door to flexibility must always be open and the mind must not be closed to new ideas and concepts. Every classical Master had his own personal journey based on his place in history and his passion for his art. All of us can learn and contribute something new which may be revealed through our time spent with our horses.

13.2 Our horses can offer a deep spiritual quality which gives our relationships and training more meaning

I am returning to the homeland of my inspiration, a country of my heart, Portugal, for a sabbatical for further study. Owning Spanish horses and having trained in Portugal, I am completely at home in Iberia and hope that our clients and friends will continue to visit us and remain an important part of our lives.

I would love to see classical training and competitive dressage being joined by a common thread of horsemanship and understanding. I believe horsemanship is the way to progress communication and leadership, together with empathy and love (Figure 13.2).

We can all strive to learn, whatever our competitive goals, and explore new boundaries leading us to deeper bonds of friendship and trust. The less talented horse may move mountains to please his rider, producing inspired work which will be an expression of his personality; this will begin to create the art.

I hope that this book will provide a source of inspiration to help you build on your individuality and that of your horse. With a desire for knowledge, together with exploration, a relationship built upon friendship may be formed; your horse can then become your soul friend and you can experience the feeling of riding from your heart.

It is important to recall Nuno Oliveira's great words, 'There can be no art without love'. Let us all aspire to producing art in our horsemanship.

Indiano XVIII studies his own reflection (photo: Bob Langrish)

Appendix

In Praise of the Iberian Horse

Every breed and type of horse has the capacity to understand the techniques of breathing taught within this book but the Iberian horse, with his particularly sensitive and highly perceptive nature, has become a particularly great teacher for me. His great intelligence and capacity for communication will be my constant guide.

The Iberian horse is, without a doubt, perfectly suited to this training philosophy, perhaps because of his tractable and gentle nature and his long-standing affinity with man. This chapter is dedicated to the relationships of the heart between human and horse, revealing the depth of love and connection between people and horses across the world.

I have been introduced to people far and wide who share an affinity with, particularly Iberian, horses and whose lives have been enriched by their love and commitment to these horses. We share a common bond of constantly searching for ways to further understand the ways of the horse whilst also teaching him to respect and trust the ways of human nature.

Historically, the Iberian horse was highly valued as the mount most sought after by the classical Masters. Both the Spanish and Portuguese have a deep-rooted passion for their horses which descend from the same early

Iberian horses. The Spanish Pure-bred is the result of not only selective breeding but also the soul of Andalusia, the area in Southern Spain still considered by many to be the spiritual home of the breed. (Figure Ap.1.)

I first became enchanted by the Iberian horse when I visited Portugal and rode Lusitano schoolmasters. I had never experienced such lightness, sensitivity or innate empathy in any other breed and I could understand why the Iberian horse was the breed preferred by the classical Masters. For centuries their bloodlines represented horses which were specifically bred to establish all these qualities. Iberian horses are now recognized around the world for their supreme athletic ability and unique trainability. Today several studs are breeding and training for the competitive dressage arena.

Ap.1 Six Spanish mares yoked (tied) together in a *cobra*. Traditionally, mares were yoked together in this way to thresh grain

Ap.2 The Royal School performing in Seville

(Figure Ap.2.) Collection comes naturally to the Iberian horse but many studs have now begun to breed a horse with more ability to extend which is proving to be attractive to the dressage competitor.

The Spanish dressage team's recent results have ensured the team and its horses a high profile around the world. Iberian horses have won medals for dressage at the Olympics and the European Championships. Evento, Invasor and Gaucho can claim international fame in the dressage arena and John Whitaker has taken his talented Lusitano stallion, Novilheiro, to the top in international showjumping.

In England, many competitive riders have often sourced their horses in Germany or Holland, but dressage is about horse and rider working as a partnership and if English riders could experience the extraordinary abilities of the Iberian horse and the rapport it is possible to establish with him, I feel confident that many more would choose an Iberian in order to enjoy not only an empathetic relationship but also competitive success.

The Iberian horse is extremely capable of taking part in many equestrian disciplines and he is a very comfortable horse for pleasure riding and side-saddle and is also used for driving. The usual height of the Iberian horse is over 15 hh and many stand between 15.2 hh and 16.2 hh. These horses can tend to look taller than their actual height as they are impressive and their conformation supports good natural self-carriage. The Iberian horse is also good across country and over fences as he has much athletic ability.

These abilities together with his natural empathy with people mean that the Iberian horse can become a much-loved partner and friend, whatever your chosen equestrian field, and people are beginning to look at the importance of this relationship, which transcends any seemingly important training goal.

The essence of this book is to provide the student with more tools of communication, thus enhancing awareness of the true nature of the horse. When we can perceive his thoughts, we can influence his responses more harmoniously.

In long-standing human relationships, a spirit of empathy can be created where one can read the thoughts of another before a word is spoken. It is wonderful to experience similar relationships with the horse, to connect with the pride and spirit he chooses to reveal to us when his training is built on trust and understanding.

In this appendix we take a look at some equine partnerships worldwide to see how the spirit of the Iberian horse will captivate and teach by touching the soul.

England

Samantha Tilley

Sam Tilley was the first person in England to introduce me to the pure-bred Spanish horse. Sam tells her story in her own words which not only relate how she first fell in love with the Spanish horse at a very young age but also how two Spanish stallions helped her through difficult times in different periods of her life.

'When I was nine years old my parents separated, which was a very traumatic time for me. I then moved to Spain with my father, stepmother and young half-sister. Each day, the goats would wander past our villa winding their way down from the hills and through the olive groves. Even then as a child I was in total awe of the flamboyant Spanish lifestyle and I fell madly in love with a black Spanish stallion who regularly passed our villa. I became totally obsessed by his beauty! I would sit out on the balcony quietly willing this stallion to come by again. My Dad grew tired of my asking to see the horse, and so he would jump in the car just to drive me to the stables. That wasn't enough for me as I then pestered my Dad to find out if I could ride the horse.

'My father had spoken to the little Spanish man who rode the stallion and one day he stopped outside our house. I could hardly believe it when he put me onto this magnificent horse. I felt like the Queen, the greatest rider in the world (Figure Ap.3) The next day we were invited to the stables where I rode this stallion around the sand school. I was hanging onto his black mane whilst he performed piaffe and passage; I thought I was in heaven! When we finished, the stallion gently bowed down so that I could get off.

'This memory lived on in my mind and back in England, twenty years later, my dream of owning one of these beautiful horses came true. In 1994 I was reading *Horse and Hound* when I saw an Andalusian stallion advertised and he was quite local to me. Having no money, it was ridiculous going to see him but I did, and came face to face with a stunning bay Andalusian stallion: Lengueto (Figure Ap.4).

'I sold everything I could, my car and my event and dressage horses, so that I could buy him. My friends thought I was mad but now they can see why I wanted him. This little horse brings joy to so many people with his characteristically gentle Spanish temperament. Everyone is allowed a cuddle; children adore him, especially little girls.

'His courage has contributed to his success in cross-country, driving and dressage competitions and he has given so much pleasure to people in a number of displays. This little stallion has won numerous prizes, too many to list here, but that is not the most important thing to me.

'Lengueto has helped me through so many traumatic times with his nobility of spirit, has become a major part of my life and he has fulfilled my childhood dream. I now breed Spanish horses, which is something I never thought I would do. He has sired beautiful progeny and many of my friends have foals by him, ensuring that his essence will live on. I owe so much to the Spanish horse, especially Lengueto.'

Ap.3 Sam on the black stallion in Spain

Ap.4 Sam and Lengueto

Nancy Nash

Nancy Nash comes from a household steeped in traditional dressage. Franz Rochowansky and Henri Cuyer were constant visitors and Lorna Johnstone, Nancy's famous mother, competed in the Munich Olympic Games and represented Great Britain in both the Mexican and Helsinki Olympics.

Nancy tells the story of her pure-bred Spanish mare, Portilla. Barrie and I first set eyes on Portilla at the stud of Yeguada Senorio de Bariain in the mountains of northern Spain where we spent some time selecting fillies who appeared to have good potential in their conformation and gaits. Portilla captured my interest as she trotted across the field with amazing freedom in her stride, showing much natural ability.

Nancy came to visit us because she was interested in the Iberian horse and consequently spent most of the day looking at some fillies and our stallions, and talking through the characteristics of the breed. Nancy continues the story in her own words.

'I first set eyes on Portilla at the home of Jenny and Barrie Rolfe who spent some time showing me their beautiful stallions and fillies. One three-year-old caught my eye, as she moved like a dream (Figure Ap.5).

'On that day I went home empty handed, but could not get the way that filly moved out of my mind. The Spanish horses were so very

Ap.5 Portilla enjoying freedom in her paddock

different from any horse I had ever trained for dressage that I felt compelled to consult various knowledgeable people about them.

'I was most interested by what I learnt and decided to buy Portilla. She arrived at the end of April and immediately became the herd leader of my two warmblood youngsters, despite the fact that they towered over her. I could see in her attitude to life why these horses were bred for fighting wars and bulls.

'I had a very experienced head lad of a racing stable back her. He was used to backing wayward youngsters and had a wonderful way with horses but Portilla was not having anyone on her back!

'Day after day he was bucked off and quietly got back on again until his perseverance won; one day Portilla simply did not buck any more and from the moment I was able to ride her, our friendship and trust began to grow.

'She has now been placed many times in dressage tests up to Elementary standard. She is certainly the most intelligent mount I have ever ridden and I have previously trained a horse to compete at International level. Portilla is now tackling flying changes, and piaffe and passage come naturally to her, whether she is ridden or at liberty. To me she is the most exciting prospect. We are looking forward to the future and already are planning the music for her competitive career which will include the freestyle dressage to music.'

Nancy's final words were tinged with sadness, as she expressed her deep sorrow, that her mother, who would have been most appreciative of Portilla's immense talent, is no longer alive to see and ride this wonderful mare.

Beverley Clark

Beverley Clark is the proud owner of Chiquita, a foal we brought over from the same stud as Delfin, that of Pedro Cardenas (Figure Ap.6). Beverley had been experiencing a few training problems with her warmblood mare and she was looking for a horse that might prove a little easier, perhaps with more lightness and trainability.

Bev had bought a book about Iberian horses and read it from cover to cover whilst in bed with flu. As a result she totally fell in love with the

Ap.6 Chiquita as a youngster

idea of owning a beautiful, sweet-tempered Spanish horse.

Chiquita had the character of her lineage, being brave, honest and sensible. She loved people but with an independence of nature. Often when Beverley dismounted after a ride, Chiquita would turn and whicker as if to say, 'Hello, I didn't know you were up there!'

Beverley sometimes enjoys just watching Chiquita as she demonstrates her heritage performing magnificent airs above the ground, playing in the field.

Beverley feels that the collected work will come easily to Chiquita in the future as she is already sensitive, very light in the mouth and easy to school. She always tries her best and appears to enjoy her work under saddle giving one hundred per cent to her work. Chiquita responds readily to the techniques of breathing and in particular Bev has found that Chiquita is lighter in the hand during transitions because of these techniques. Chiquita used to lean on the hand during transitions but now works in better balance; in fact she will go from walk to canter in response to just a breath.

Bev's warmblood mare, Artiste, would sometimes be tense and not listen to her rider at all but when Bev used the breathing techniques in all transitions, Artiste began to feel less resistant.

Bev says of her, 'She started to listen to me and calmed down after a little while. I tried using these breathing techniques several times when she became tense and it worked; although, as a rider, I have to discipline myself to remember to do it as it is easy to forget!

'If I use the discipline to calm myself, I then seem to influence Artiste and she begins to listen to my aids. It definitely calms her down and she tunes in to me. I am using the techniques most of the time now for transitions and am finding her much rounder, lighter in the hand and more submissive during transitions; in fact I can give the inside hand completely during both upwards and downwards transitions.

'One day she was responding to me so well that I achieved a halt to canter transition with a breath. I use the breathing techniques a lot with her for walk to canter transitions and they definitely stop her getting so wound up and tense.'

Beverley says of her Spanish mare, 'She is a joy to own! I would happily fill my yard with these paragons of virtue'. Well, her dreams may come true, as Beverley has just bought our lovely filly Ebanista and in the future hopes to breed really good quality Spanish horses with temperaments and gaits to match.

Gill Kennerley

My friend Gill Kennerley is a well-known classical trainer in the U.K. who previously trained as a professional ballet dancer. Gill says that her dancing has given her more of an appreciation of the Spanish horse and his ability to perform and adds that the Iberian horses are so sensitive, soft and rounded in their backs and gifted with the ability to collect naturally or, you might say, 'dance'.

As a classical dressage trainer and rider, Gill finds that the Iberian horses are wonderful school-masters. Once a rider has learned the basic technique and has achieved balance they can absorb each stride with the pelvis. Because of the sensitivity of this breed, Iberian horses help to show the rider how to ride in harmony and aid further development of mind and body awareness.

Gill's special once-in-a-lifetime horse is a Lusitano (Portuguese) stallion Rouxinol, who holds a very special place

Ap.7 Gill riding Rouxinol

in her heart (Figure Ap.7). She says, 'He gives me so much pleasure and is both an exciting and beautiful horse to watch. He is highly sensitive and aloof but talented and proud. He was owned and trained by a strong male Portuguese rider and was used to work cattle.'

Rouxinol, needed to be brave, alert and very sharp, obeying his rider at all times, because of the dangers he could encounter when working the bulls. He was a tremendous challenge and over several years he took Gill on a wonderful journey, which proved to be a steep learning curve. He has become a talented classical dressage horse and a fantastic horse to ride. He is Gill's soul mate: obedient, trusting and sincere.

This reminds me so much of my relationship with Delfin and I feel Gill's stallion has offered her a similar desire for friendship, along with an amazing learning experience. We share a common empathy having been taught by the most sensitive and intelligent of horses.

Lucy Nicolayson

Lucy is a skilled musician who teaches the art of playing the piano. I first met Lucy after several discussions about the possibility of her finding an Iberian stallion with whom she could learn to train with a more in-depth understanding of his nature. She decided to spend some time with us learning about the importance of body language and the way we can relate to the horse.

Lucy says, 'I remember the day my beautiful Spanish stallion, Floyd, arrived from Spain. We had been waiting two days more than anticipated for his arrival, and I had driven down to Devon the night before, not having any idea when he would actually arrive. I drove to Jenny's farm to see what preparations I could make, and there he was; he had just arrived in the lorry. My first contact with him that day also triggered my first real lesson about communicating with him. Being very relieved that he had finally arrived, I remember holding his lead rope tight near his chin to take him to his stable. I also remember the feeling of him resisting my pull, although we did get to the stable!

'It was only later when Jenny mentioned in a different context how important it is to always 'invite' a stallion to do something, thereby initiating a communication, that the difference between pulling Floyd somewhere and asking him to come with me became clear in my mind. I have since been aware of this difference in feeling many times in my contact with him. Whenever I have truly invited him to do something and given him the time to respond, I have invariably been rewarded with lightness and understanding from him.

'In lungeing and loose work, one of the things I learnt with Jenny was to breathe out distinctly as a signal to move forward or to liven up the movement, and to breathe in to slow down. Floyd always responds. I believe that breathing is perceived by him as part of the whole picture, the other part being my body language, which naturally changes with the changes in breathing. When the situation is one in which he is very focused and we work closely together in a small space, he will respond to the most subtle of signals; a light inward breath, which then naturally instigates the small degree of straightening in my body, will gain his immediate response. Equally, when I am riding him, if we are "in synch", he will mirror my breathing in with slowing down and move forward when the tension is released in my body as I breathe out. (Figures Ap.8 and Ap.9.)

'I think that the way one breathes in any particular moment mirror's one state of mind and, conversely, one can alter one's state of mind by the way one controls breathing.

'One of the things that I often have to deal with is how to establish guidelines that respect the horse's nature but allow things to work my way as well. People often say that horses have to be "controlled" but I think it is more important to ask how is it possible to motivate a horse to want to try to please you? Everything will then be made easier and everyone wins.

'With regard to these ideas, a couple of things Jenny had said to me about working with Floyd in his stable were inspirational. I had allowed Floyd to wander around his stable sometimes while I was grooming him as it seemed to me it was rather a long time to ask him to stand still. Naturally he was very interested in what was going on outside and so he kept going to the door where I could not reach him properly to groom him. After a few days this became annoying and I had to admit to myself that the problem was that I had been inconsistent in what I had been asking for but I didn't like to nag him constantly.

Ap.8 Lucy with her friend Floyd

'To help me resolve the problem, Jenny gave me a solution, one that he would enjoy. I had to continually change my body position to block him as soon as he moved to take a step forward, when I had asked him to stand. He began to respond very quickly, became attentive and we were learning the art of communication together. Since that time, I feel so much pleasure when we communicate well and he responds with pride and obedience.'

Ap.9 Lucy using subtle communication to gain Floyd's attention

The USA

Lanys Kane-Eddie

Gremlan Farm was established in 1979 by Lanys Kane-Eddie. This was the beginning of a quest to further her knowledge of the genetics, genealogy and history of the Spanish Pure-bred horse

Lanys has over many years built up a strong reputation for breeding and sourcing the most talented and beautiful of horses which began with the importation to America of Regalado II, a son of the legendary stallion Leviton. This sensational stallion competed to Prix St. Georges level on the open dressage circuit, where he attracted many spectators who just enjoyed the pleasure of watching this beautiful and talented horse.

Indiano XVIII is the foundation stallion for the Gremlan stud farm (Figure Ap.10). He is so beautiful with great presence and nobility and a coat that shimmers pearly white. He was initially exported from Spain to Mexico before Lanys became successful in her mission to acquire him as her foundation stallion for the Gremlan stud. This magnificent horse was

Ap.10 Indiano XVIII, the foundation stallion of the Gremlan stud

successful in winning gold medals in Spain, Mexico and America, and so he has truly found a position as a world-class representative of his breed.

Lanys is a classical dressage rider and she writes articles on the pure-bred Spanish horse describing it as the breed of the future for the dressage arena. With the breed being that most appreciated and prized by the classical Masters, this would appear to be a realistic vision.

Lanys feels that the Spanish horse is a combination of true strength with soundness. He is short-coupled which makes him outstanding as an athlete and also 'the Master of collection'.

In Holland, *Horse International* magazine recently published the official listings of leading dressage sires and Lanys can be justifiably proud to have bred Navarre GF, the first Spanish stallion to be placed in the top five. This happened just once during the tabulation of competitive scores but this does mean we are on the crest of a wave and that the future of dressage may not be dominated by warmbloods; both the Spanish and Lusitano horses are demonstrating untapped talent for future competition success.

Navarre GF is the sire of Gorron GF who is now ridden by the well-known international dressage rider, Janne Rumbough.

Janne Rumbough

Janne has committed much of her life to international competition and with her very famous stallion, Gaucho III, has totally captivated all who have watched her partnership with this legendary horse. Gaucho was bred by Yeguada Senorio de Bariain and had won many prizes in Spain before Janne imported him to America (Figure Ap.11). He has an incredible personality combined with beauty and amazing gaits. Barrie and I are proud to have Gaucho's beautiful dark bay son, Maestu, at our stud.

When Janne had her sights set on the Olympic team, she and Gaucho succeeded in being chosen for the pre-selection trials but, very sadly, he sustained an injury which prevented him for further international success but his personality and tremendous talent had already made his reputation legendary. He won the USDF gold medal and many FEI classes. Gaucho now demonstrates his talents at displays and recently held the captivated audience totally spellbound at the Fiesta Festival in Florida.

Ap.11 Janne Rumbough on Gaucho III with Alvaro Muguruza and his brother of Yeguada Senorio de Bariain

Janne says of Gaucho, 'He is such a special horse and always a gentleman; he is a class act to handle, never pushy and he is always so intelligent both to handle and ride. Gaucho is a natural showman. He was born this way! The crowd always inspires him and he will rise to the occasion and gives of all his pride and personality.'

Canada

Muriel Chestnut

Muriel Chestnut lives in Ontario, Canada and is the proud owner of Soberbio XII, a stunning dark bay stallion from the stud of Villa Mazarra, Barcelona, Spain (Figure Ap.12). Muriel tells her own story.

'When I first laid eyes on Soberbio, standing quietly, tied to a pillar outside in the courtyard of the Villa Mazzara, I remember my heart climbing into my throat and not being able to hold back the tears of joy and disbelief that I was actually in the presence of my dream horse! He has the perfect body type, solid without any heaviness and the most romantically elegant neck I have ever seen on a horse. It was like being

Ap.12 Rosa Llobet riding Soberbio

in the presence of greatness and feeling rather unworthy. He was, and still is, completely docile, especially for a young stallion, and never bites, nips, kicks or gives me any reason to worry.

'Soberbio has the most calm disposition which is very conducive to soothing me; we really have a Yin Yang relationship. Under saddle he is a luxury sports car: easy to handle, yet power to burn. He has what Charles de Kunffy describes as a "body

trot", i.e. every leg has a job and they compete for attention. He is utterly remarkable to watch too. Soberbio is one of those rare horses that may come along just once in a lifetime. I am truly blessed to have this horse.

'Soberbio has become my soul mate and I'm so looking forward to the future and learning all this beautiful stallion can teach to me. I know now, that my belief in him was warranted and that the sacrifice was completely worth it.

'This is how I can describe the experience of my lovely stallion Soberbio finding me. You see I wasn't looking for a horse at the time. In fact I had been precisely instructed by my husband not to even think about it! We already had a small herd of ponies, young horses and a couple of broodmares, and now was definitely *not* the time to be considering another horse. But after selling my Prix St. Georges mare several years back, I hadn't had a "good" horse to ride in some time.

'The hard part was justifying purchasing this young stallion to my family: "Where is the money going to come from and what makes you think that you really *need* this horse? Is this a good enough reason for you to buy him?"

'These were legitimate questions and I didn't exactly have the answers but, boy, I bet there isn't a Pit Bull or Jack Russell out there that had a more ferocious determination than I.

'I looked at it this way (and tried to convince the non-horsey but crucial people involved); it was like the old Masters who, at a point in their careers needed to create their own paints from the best raw materials available. They needed (yes, *needed*) to create specific tones and colours and textures that no one else had ever created. These paints were a direct function of the artists' own ability and the availability of the necessary raw materials, without which the ideal colours and textures could not be possible. The same is true with the coming together of the right combination of horse and rider in order to produce a masterpiece. Put painting-by-numbers paints in the hands of Monet and we wouldn't have the magical paintings that we so treasure today.

'My Soberbio is an inspiration to me every day. Everyone who has met him has been in awe of him. I know we were meant to share our lives, although it was probably the most difficult thing I had to do, emotionally as well as physically; I felt in my heart, it would all be worth it in the end.

'I have a great friend and mentor in Frank Grelo. He is a classically trained Portuguese gentleman, a student of Nuno Oliveira and a true artist on horseback (or on the ground for that matter). Frank has a wonderful saying that rings in my head, "There is no love without sacrifice".'

Spain

Over many years Barrie and I have been fortunate to meet some of the most charming people in our lives. They are the owners and breeders of the Spanish Pure-bred horses in their native Spain. The enthusiasm of these people for their horses is totally infectious, as is their love of hospitality and friendship. Some of our warmest memories are of the times spent under the intense glow of Spanish sunshine, looking at magnificent colts being taken through their paces. The background of flamenco guitar and an aura of fiesta make for lasting impressions which will be with us always.

I spent a lot of time sourcing the bloodlines for their qualities of trainability, personality, beauty and gaits. Llanys from the Gremlan stud was a guiding light as she directed me towards the stud of Villa Mazzara in Northern Spain.

Silvia Mazzara

Silvia Mazzara lives near Barcelona and has built up a stud around top show and dressage bloodlines. Her resident stallion is Ebanisto, who is a living legend in Spain (Figure Ap.14). Silvia has bred many leading stallions, but Ebanisto is outstanding as both Champion of Spain and France. His amazing movement has meant that his stock is highly prized around the world with many being exported to the USA.

Silvia describes Ebanisto in a way that so aptly sums up the spirit of our Spanish horses: Through our stud several stallions have passed, all of good lines of blood and with many awards, but the greatness of this horse is very difficult to explain; his presence is a mixture of charm, elegance and potency. He is very sensitive and very balanced. It is easy to recognize his stock within a group of foals; he transmits an extraordinary

Ap.14 Ebanisto, a legend in Spain

Ap.15 A *cobra* of mares from the Villa Mazzara Stud

movement, elegant heads and necks, strong shoulder. To me is difficult to be impartial with Ebanisto. Maybe you would consider it silliness, but if you look at his eyes you can understand the greatness of this horse.'

Silvia' words have been echoed many times over, as an expression of love for the Spanish horse (Figure Ap.15).

Our lovely young filly Ebanista, a daughter of Ebanisto, is a prime example of trainability and is now owned by Bev Clark. Ebanista came into the school for the first time as a three-year-old to do some loose work with me. Within ten minutes she had settled down and was responding to my breathing and body language. We had some clients in the school who were amazed by her quick responses. They had previously been watching Delfin who responds to every small change in my breathing and body language. Jokingly they commented that Ebanista would also soon be understanding the lateral work, just like Delfin.

I responded to their comments by moving my body to ask for a lateral movement; Ebanista immediately tuned into my body language and

Ap.16 Seni-Regenta at home on the farm

Ap.17 Ebano, our most beautiful kind son of Ebanisto

performed a few strides of leg yield, just for fun. She was so happy to learn and demonstrate the true spirit and nature of this breed. These horses appear to yearn for a connection with people.

Our treasured mare Seni-Regenta has won major awards in Spain for movement and her aristocratic beauty is outstanding (Figure Ap.16). She has breath-taking charisma and presence and, as with our other fillies, was chosen after much time spent researching the genetic and stud histories. She is in foal this year to the great Ebanisto. We, and the many other breeders around the world, feel this breed can not only be a great sports horse, but also a companion, friend and soul mate to be treasured and loved.

Jenny and Delfin

I have a new young stallion: Ebano is a magnificent three-year-old colt, the beautiful kind son of Ebanisto. Ebano will help to formulate the future (Figure Ap.17).

Index